The Green Historical Walking Guide to Bradford

Mark Alexander Jackson

This book is dedicated to Lou Parson, the most fantastic Jack Russell any man can ever hope to share his life with.

All the walks contained within this Historical Walking guide can be completed using only public transport therefore making it "Green" and ethical.

CW01496699

The Stag's Head Publishing Company (Queensbury)

ISBN: 9798621858384

Forward

I have always enjoyed walking and dabbling in history of one kind or another. More years ago than I can remember I completed an A level course in Modern International History at Bradford College, but I found that local history is more appealing and inspiring than matters involving The Schlieffen Plan, the advent of The League of Nations or the rise of Adolf Hitler.

Merge together walking and local history and it almost becomes an addiction. One can connect with this type of history. You can see it, feel it, breathe it and immerse yourself in it.

These walks were planned with military precision using Google Earth, old Ordnance Survey maps dating back over 150 years, and my sometimes lucid and vivid imagination. I used the great local bus services for all my travels as I refuse to own or drive one of those new-fangled motor vehicle things any longer.

I love the sense of personal freedom this affords me and besides the old man with the big white beard upstairs didn't give us legs for nowt you know.

Contents

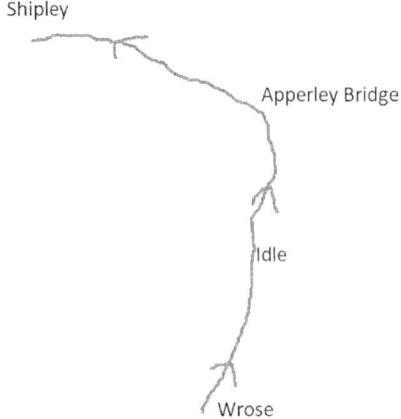

This walk is just an ideal way to blow away the cobwebs as the first part is practically all downhill and the second part involves an easy stroll along the level confines of the Leeds to Liverpool canal. Nothing complicated just a fairly simple linear stroll down through the village of Idle and then along the Canal before ending at Shipley.

Any number of buses will drop you at the Five Lane Ends roundabout or thereabouts (612/633/747) The approximate distance for this walk is 4.0 miles.

From the Five Lanes Ends roundabout you make your way down Bradford towards the village of Idle. Almost immediately you pass by the former Jowett car factory which is now, of course, a William Morrison's supermarket on your right.

Jowett's had begun as a company elsewhere in Bradford in 1901 and was founded by the brothers Benjamin and William Jowett. They were among the early pioneers of car manufacturing in Britain, with the emphasis being on the production of light, affordable cars.

The company moved to the Springfield Works site in Idle in 1919 and, for the next 35 years cars and vans were produced there, including many that have become collectors' items since.

Many models of cars and vans were made at the factory. Amongst them was the Kestrel, the Ken, the Jupiter and the Javelin, and these still evoke fond memories among car enthusiasts. After the Second World War the company was sold, but by the mid-1950s, it was in financial difficulties. Jowett's stopped making cars at the Idle factory in 1954, but continued in business for a while, making aircraft parts and spare parts for Jowett's vehicles at a site elsewhere in Yorkshire.

However, the Idle site was sold to Harvester International who produced tractors there until the early 1980s. The factory was demolished in 1983 and the site is now a large retail park dominated by the supermarket and a drive-in MacDonald's.

A little further down Bradford Road you pass The Springfield pub on your right, and immediately after you see a street that runs down the side of the pub- this is Arthur Street. This still partially cobbled track once led to quite a sizable concern named Friar Mill.

Back on the main road, you make your way past where the old railway line once crossed on its way towards nearby Idle Railway Station.

Idle Railway Station opened on 15 April 1875 and was situated south of the High Street (to the left as you now stand), next to the Oddfellows Hall. This building predates the railway station as it was originally built in 1840. Passenger service on the Great Northern Railway loop line ceased on 2 February 1931 and the passenger station closed. Goods traffic continued on the whole line until October 1964 and between Shipley and Idle until 1968.

Little now remains to show that there was ever a railway station in Idle. The station was just south of the bridge where the railway crossed High Street at the junction with New Street. It then followed the route of what is now Idlecroft Road south towards Eccleshill to the right as you now stand.

The historic village of Idle is located to the north of Bradford and to the East of Shipley. The place-name Idle probably relates to the Old English term Idel meaning an empty place or an uncultivated area. In 1583-4, the Manor is portrayed as containing mostly uncultivated land and woodland, with some quarries for wall stones and slates.

Idle lordship comprised the settlements of Idle, Thorpe, Wrose, and Windhill. Open fields were situated immediately south and west of Idle with Thackley Common, and the East and West Woods to the north. Idle Mill, comprising a water corn mill and a fulling mill with two stocks, stood on the south bank of the River Aire, the river forming the northern bounds of the lordship.

Moorland and the hamlet of Wrose, with its fields systems, were situated on the south and southwest bounds of the estate. Industrial activity in this period included The Iron Smithies, powered by a water mill situated to the southwest of Windhill, on the east side of Bradford Beck. Earlier industries included tanning as did many areas of Bradford during this period.

The Inhabitants of Idle comprised twenty-one tenants and fourteen cottages, the majority of tenants each residing in smallholdings or farmsteads consisting of a house, barn, and outbuildings, with a croft or parcel of land to the rear of the property. The cottagers' lived in a cottage with a garden and had rights of Common Land.

Around 1837 Idle was a populous clothing village with a long main street. A number of scribbling and fulling mills and a few worsted mills were situated within the general area; a cattle market was established at Idle in 1836. The Settlement had mostly remained clustered around the five routes leading to the village and the increase of population and industrial activity, including Union Mill (Woollen) and Castle Mills (Worsted), had been absorbed in development to the south and east of the original village core.

The growth of industry and population resulted in the opening of a railway station. The Great Northern Railway operated the first passenger train to Idle in 1875. This station closed in 1931 with the line finally closing in 1968. The station, bridge, and tracks were dismantled in 1972 and replaced by Idlecroft Road.

Continuing down along the main road, you soon pass The Brewery Tap public house on your left and immediately after this point turn left down Croft Street, noticing the tiny disused Wesleyan Methodist graveyard to your left. This piece of consecrated ground stands right at the side of the road in front of a beautiful row of 18th century former weaver's cottages. Looking sadly neglected today it contains one Commonwealth War grave behind its locked gates.

Passing by more rows of similar cottages you turn right onto Apperley Road and head towards the former coaching inn known today as The George Inn.

Leaving The George you continue to head towards the canal. Before long you pass by the late 18th century, Grade II listed former Miln Holme Farm on the right before arriving at Milman Swing Bridge.

Built in 1810 and formally named Kitman Bridge, this canal swing bridge is surrounded by a grouping of mainly Grade II listed cottages originally built for canal workers. Alongside these cottages there was a series of three wharves and one of only four maintenance yards on the whole Leeds-Liverpool canal. One of the cottages, built in 1776 served as the Toll House for the bridge.

A short walk in the direction of Apperley Bridge is the marina. Built on the site of the former canal basin, this is one of the few marinas on the whole canal. The basin served Oaklea Mills, a three-storey former Worsted mill constructed in 1896.

Today the marina is used as a housing point for a number of canal houseboats and has its own Chandler shop which sells all manner of items for use by people enjoying the life of a canal boat owner.

From this point you now start along the canal towards Shipley and cross over to the other towpath by way of the swing bridge. The howling of the dogs from the kennels alongside the far bank may be music to your ears or perhaps not depending on your views. Just past the kennels the fields lie flat and run right down to the bank. Horses graze lazily here in the early summer sun safe in the knowledge that the humans and dogs on the far bank cannot trouble them.

In a few short minutes you will reach Dobson Lock. This traditional and well-kept Grade II listed lock was constructed in 1777 with its adjacent canal company warehouse alongside and raises the canal by some twenty feet. The former warehouse was converted into three beautiful cottages one of which today houses a British Waterways office. Mount the top of the lock at this point to look over the fields towards the estate of Esholt and Rawdon beyond.

Just beyond the lock is a workshop and fitting area for the various maintenance tasks that British Waterways have to carry on out this stretch of the canal. It may be a hive of activity with all manner of trucks and vans parked alongside. Walking on for a short distance you soon reach Bottom Farm and its quaint tearoom (if it is still open). This is the only place on this stretch of the canal where weary travellers can take refreshment.

Up ahead you will see the twin iron riveted railway bridges that cross the canal at this point. The line was constructed in 1846 as the Bradford-Shipley-Leeds line with just the nearside and oldest bridge being built at this time. The railway was extended in the early 20th century from two lines to four and this necessitated the widening of a tunnel, embankment and the construction of the second bridge.

Some time afterwards the older pair of lines closed, the rails were removed and the Southern bridge was allowed to deteriorate. As you pass underneath the remaining bridge look above and marvelled at the thousands of rivets in their perfect uniform lines. Painted in a dark colour the bridge looks as though it had been built only the day before.

Across on the far bank, the flat meadows has now given way to dense woodland. This is Dawson Wood, which was once part of the privately-owned Esholt Estate and contains trees of many species and ages, most going back hundreds of years. Here on the still water's surface there may be a pair of Ducks followed by their family of Ducklings. Mum and Dad teaching their children all about life on the water.

The canal continues to wind and snake its way past the woods as you approach Esholt Sewage plant. The smell at this point depends on which way the breeze is blowing.

The woods on the far bank has now become so dense now that it appears almost impenetrable to all creatures but the resident animals. Hollins Wood gives way to Field Wood then this area becomes the famous Buck Wood. Here you pass underneath the rusting steel structure of the former narrow-gauge bridge which once carried the Sewage plant railway over the canal and into Buck Wood.

On the Thackley side of the canal at this point is Yorkshire Water's stormwater tanks and wastewater screening plant. Nearby is another magnificent set of canal locks named Field Locks. A 3-rise lock constructed in 1774-77 and designed by the engineers James Brindley and John Longbotham this structure comprises three adjoining wide chambers of coursed dressed stone with stone coping, the walls of the upper two curving out at their tails, with stone steps to either side.

The lock consists of two pairs of late 20th-century wooden gates to the top chamber with one pair of the same to each of the lower ones. Each pair has integral rack and pinion paddle gearing and adjacent boxed ground paddles, with the exception of the middle chamber, where the ground paddles have been removed. Each chamber has a wooden plank footbridge across its tail. There is an overflow weir to offside from the towpath, with channels leading into it from two lower chambers.

The canal towpath winds onwards towards Shipley between the now dense Buck Wood on your left and a thinner stretch of wood leading down to the River Aire on the nearside. Buck Wood lies to the north of Thackley and covers an area of fairly level high ground, as well as the steep north-facing slope down to the Leeds and Liverpool canal. Above this valley, Buck Wood forms a broad semi-circular zone of woodland, adjoining other similar woods that are part of a woodland corridor stretching along the Aire Valley. Covering 42 hectares, this wood is bordered by the curving route of the canal at its lower perimeter around 60 m above sea-level. Its highest boundary 135 m above sea level, is shaped by the tree-lined sweep of Ainsbury Avenue leading from Thackley through to Esholt.

Buck Wood lies above a layer of millstone grit rock with numerous rocky outcrops, especially on the steeper slopes, where quarrying has taken place. The wood contains a mixture of habitats, with areas of both broad-leaved woodland and mixed deciduous and coniferous plantations. It has patches of marshland created by the many springs occurring throughout the Wood.

There are fields scattered within the woodland, some used as pasture for grazing. With its variety of habitats, it is an important reservoir for wildlife in Thackley and the surrounding area, and an area for walking and other leisure activities.

As you stand next to Buck Mill Bridge, look down to your right towards the river. This was the site of a quite sizable and longstanding mill of the same name. Situated between the canal and the River Aire, the mill belonged to the Lord of the Manor, and everyone in the area was required to take their corn to the mill for grinding. Some of the tracks and paths that exist today were probably formed by generations of local people carrying their annual harvest of grain to the Mill to be ground into flour.

The Lord of the Manor received rent from the miller who was his tenant, and the charge for grinding the corn provided income for the miller. It is also recorded that as early as 1567 the Mill had diversified, and was also being used for processing woollen cloth. By 1584, the corn and fulling mills and the house attached to it were occupied by the Buck family, which led to the Mill becoming known as Buck Mill. At that date, they also held various pieces of land nearby and by the mid-eighteenth century the Mill no longer had a monopoly for grinding corn, so the emphasis of its production changed towards the wool trade, as part of Bradford's rapidly increasing primary industry.

The Stansfield family rebuilt the Mill around 1800, adding a scribbling mill to the corn and fulling mill. Benjamin Thornton, who also owned Bowling Green Mill in Thackley and Albion Mill in Idle, rented Buck Mill in the 1860s. He built a new warehouse and wool-washing room, which consisted of two large four-storey blocks, along with a boiler house, engine, and chimney.

By this time the machinery was powered by steam rather than a water wheel. To conserve water for the boiler a dam was made in a field across from the mill. The remains of this can still be seen as a rectangular shape in the field on the opposite side of Buck Mill Lane.

By 1905, the Mill was described as 'Disused' on official maps. For some years before the 1914-18 War, the mill was empty and becoming increasingly derelict. Finally, in 1923, the buildings were blown up and a quantity of the stone was used to pave Buck Mill Lane which climbs the hill to Thackley.

Foundation stones of the mill complex are still visible but are now more or less completely overgrown, and the area has become unsafe because of long term problems with water leakage from the canal directly above. When the river level is low it is possible to see some early stonework and elements of the goit and its construction.

As you stand at this point on the bridge, something else may catch your attention. Across the canal from the towpath lies the narrow and cobbled Buck Mill Lane. Only a short distance up the lane stands an old cottage on the left. This secluded and romantic building sits quietly amongst the trees atop a short banking a few yards from the lane. The cottage is located up a setted footpath and was once two dwellings which shared the central corniced chimneystack. The house retains a stone roof, indicating its construction in the first half of the 19th century, although traditional window details are absent. It is quite a large cottage built of local gritstone and it stands within a clearing in the trees.

The cottage formally served as a Dog sanctuary and a report from the local Bradford newspaper The Telegraph and Argus dated 11th April 2014 said "The man behind Buck Wood Animal Sanctuary in Bradford was found dead at his home surrounded by his dogs. Alan Littlewood, 69, was discovered by police after a friend became concerned because she had been unable to contact him by phone. Long-time friend Sue Wood, of Doncaster, told the newspaper how she had been receiving daily texts from Mr Littlewood but these had ended causing her to alert the police. "He told me he was not very well and that he was going to send me a text every day. For about three days up to April 1, I hadn't heard anything. I kept texting him back but my gut instinct was that something was wrong. I rang the police to say I am very concerned about this man who lives in an isolated cottage." she said.

Mr Littlewood was found dead, laid on the settee in the kitchen with his three dogs. A post-mortem examination revealed Mr Littlewood died of pneumonia and died alone in his cottage. He ran the dog rescue operation for more than twenty years and funded it out of his own pocket. A kind and compassionate man, a man who loved his animals and his dogs.

Leaving the cottage behind you continue the short distance along the canal towards Shipley. A thousand yards further on you arrive at the site of the long-demolished Canal Tavern. This is opposite Thackley West Wood and on your right between the canal and the river. Immediately beyond this point the towpath passes the site of the former Airedale Iron Works.

From here the canal-side scenery changes from a pastoral to an industrial setting. It really was a veritable hive of activity with small quarries and ironworks sited all around this area with Dockfield Road as its centre.

Small industrial units gave way to the massive Junction Mills. This gargantuan building was constructed in several phases with the earliest section being built alongside the canal. It is here where The Bradford Canal branched off from the Leeds-Liverpool canal to make its short two-mile journey to the basin in Bradford city centre.

This short canal closed in 1922 and the junction spur is stagnant, overgrown and littered today. Beside is the derelict and forlorn Junction House, a former Toll House and warehouse. Built in 1774 this building had two gable end loading doors but is set back from the canal bank so it would appear that cargo would have been brought onto the bank before being hoisted inside for storage.

Alongside Junction House and across the canal is the beautiful and famous Junction Bridge. Constructed in 1774 this Grade II listed single-arch bridge with a stone walkway screams packhorse at you. Visions of labouring, sweating beasts piled high with bales of cloth fill your mind as you pass beneath it on your way towards Shipley. This area has seen some development in recent years with a block of fine canal-side apartments opposite Junction Mills being the most noteworthy. The view from the balconies whilst sipping Prosecco must be invigorating.

Shipley town centre is now looming in the middle distance as you pass over the point where Bradford Beck drains into the River Aire below you. The journey that begins as a series of small streams and individual becks in the high hills surrounding Bradford ends here. Notice the tiny cottage aside Gallows Bridge a short distance from here. This early 18th-century cottage sits snugly alongside the canal towpath.

The area around Gallows Bridge itself was once home to several wood-framed mills. Hence the name "Gallows" and contrary to local legend it has nothing to do with the apparatus for hanging people.

Here you cross over the small footbridge, turn right and walk the short distance along Briggate to the bus stop where you can catch the 633 or 612 bus back to Bradford Interchange.

Eldwick Bottom to Tong Park Via Baildon Moor

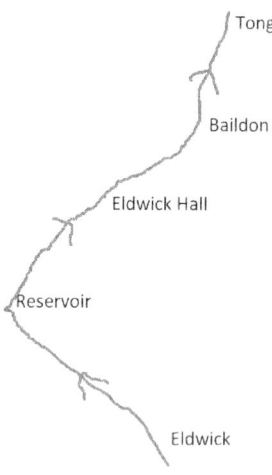

This walk begins at Eldwick Beck Bottom and this spot is reached by catching the 616 bus from Bradford Interchange. The walk itself is fairly easy going and the approximate distance is 3.50 miles.

Eldwick Bottom is an ancient hollow between two small hills and was originally a bridging point over Eldwick Beck with no permanent settlement surrounding it. The enclosure of the land around Eldwick Hall was created in the late 16th century. Eldwick Spring Farm, originally established in 1588 dates from this time. At this time, the only building on the valley floor was Eldwick Beck Mill. Built in 1800 this mill was for a short time used for Scribbling (the processing of raw fleeces) but converted to use as a corn mill in 1828. The building of this mill provided the impetus for further development. Cottages were constructed as well as a Wesleyan Methodist Church and Sunday school.

Once on the ground you proceed to walk the short distance along The Green in the direction of the magnificent Compensation Reservoir. Almost immediately you arrive at The Acorn Inn.

Built in 1820 this fully licensed inn, with accommodation for guests and lodgers was used for a time around 1841 to house Navvies who were working on the construction of the nearby reservoir.

Towards the end of the 19th century it also became a popular destination for workers from the industrial centre of nearby Bradford to enjoy the local scenery. Resisting the lure of a pint of well-kept locally brewed ale you move on towards the old packhorse trail that follows the length of Eldwick Beck towards Tewet House and the famed "Paved Causeway".

The Green is a well surfaced and smooth road with a gentle ascent which after a short distance turns steeper and into a much rougher cobbled narrow track that was obviously a packhorse trail in the past. Pause for breath here and admire the vista across the undulating fields towards the majestic Compensation Reservoir. Turning to the right to join The Monks Way, as the paved causeway was once known, you now start to ascend down the well-worn and weathered flat stones that had been used in centuries past by Medieval religious men and many others. Flanked on either side by high stout dry stone walls the track undulates up and down like a roller coaster till you reach the Eldwick Beck overflow from the reservoir.

As you pass by the reservoir you may notice the many signs warning against swimming in the cold and algae ridden water. Across the fields in the distance, you will see the outline of Eldwick Hall which you will soon pass on your way back to Eldwick Bottom after joining Otley Road.

Eldwick Hall is a Grade II listed house at Lane Head. The Hall is initialled and dated "R L 1696" (Richard Longbottom) but the first-floor doorway to the right bears the inscription "IHS 1716". Built of dressed gritstone with a stone slate roof, Eldwick Hall combines classical features with the local vernacular style. It was once reputedly owned by The Knights of Jerusalem who gave shelter and food from here to weary travellers.

On the front of the hall are thirteen stone steps that once led to an isolated chamber where food and water were provided. In 1755, a Lisbon banker named Benjamin Harboyne saw his home and fortune swallowed up by an earthquake. The shock affected him to such a degree that he became a raving madman. He was brought back to England and spent the rest of his days in chains at Eldwick Hall.

Walking back down Otley Road towards Eldwick Bottom you pass by the farmstead of Crag Top before reaching a small long-deserted Sandstone quarry. This quarry provided slabs of Sandstone for local buildings before being abandoned in the late 18th century. Today it is overgrown with Larch and Birch trees and tracts of dense vegetation. Quarries such as this are situated all over the Bradford area and are evidence of the past industrial endeavours of hard-working Bradford people.

You soon reach Spring Lane and turn left along here to make your way along the valley floor and climb up through open moorland in the direction of Baildon. This section of Spring Lane, running from Eldwick Beck to Glovershaw was repaired and widened to 7-8 yards in 1777, suggesting it was a route of some importance, and perhaps like Green Lane it was used by packhorses. Carry on towards the site of the former Eldwick Beck Mill which today has been converted into private houses. The mill pond on your right still remains and is home to a collection of brightly coloured ducks in a peaceful setting.

As Spring Lane becomes Glovershaw Lane it winds gently uphill towards the moor and contains no pavement. Along here you should stop for a while at the side of an ancient old stone roadside drinking trough and listened intently to the trickle of Eldwick Spring as it fills the void before running off under the road.

In medieval times, Baildon Moor and indeed much of this area contained Ironstone pits and small Iron Smelting works. Evidence of early Iron smelting works has been found at Glovershaw Beck and Load Pit Beck. Some evidence of ancient iron smelting was discovered alongside Glovershaw Beck just above Hope farm.

Passing by numerous quaint old 18th-century cottages and farmsteads you wind your way along Glovershaw Lane past Low Gate towards the site of the last working coal pit on Baildon Moor at Lobley Gate. This deep shaft mine closed in 1863 due to excessive flooding. We were now at the foot of an area known as Windy Hill. This area once contained many small coal pits and also numerous ancient cup and ring marked rocks. The faint outline of distant Dobrubben caravan site comes into view as you tramp along the moorland road.

The area to the left of what is now Bingley Road is taken up by part of Baildon Golf Course. You soon reach Acrehowe Hill, the site of both an ancient Prehistoric Tumulus and a stone cross. The curious remains of the Tumulus earthworks are discernible in the grassland to the left-hand side of the road just by the small car park. This is a loose double-ring of stones, fifty feet across, surrounded by a shallow trench which was most notable on the south and east sides. Two urns were also uncovered in the 1800s near the centre of the ring, nearly two feet down, containing the cremated remains of Iron Age people.

The stone cross was on the other side of the road from the prehistoric circle. This old cross was destroyed sometime in the first half of the 19th century by one of the stewards to the Lady of the Manor of Baildon, a Mr Walker. The cross was erected (probably between the 12th and 14th centuries) amidst a cluster of heathen burials and cup-and-rings, many of which would have been known by local peasants as having old lore or superstitions about them.

Dodging the errant flying golf balls, you carry on along Bingley road to reach a disused small Millstone Grit quarry named Eaves Crag on your left. Here you could spend some time searching amongst the rocks for one single rock at ground level that is marked with a Prehistoric cup and ring symbol.

Directly across the road stand three Victorian reservoirs. These reservoirs, on a 3.5-acre site, were built in the 1850s by Baildon Urban District Council Water Works to provide the village with fresh water. The village had one of the highest death rates in the country because of water-borne diseases and up to twenty-five households would use the same toilet. Two of the three structures are devoid of water and have been partially stripped of their stonework. The third contains some water and this allows the superb craftsmanship of the Victorian engineers and stonemasons to be seen inside. Sadly the reservoirs have become somewhat of a financial liability for their owners Baildon Golf Club and are earmarked for demolition and further redevelopment

From the reservoirs, you continue to walk on along Bingley Road before crossing over Hawksworth Road and then continuing along Moorside. This track skirts along the edge of the disused Low Eaves Delf on your left, from which high-quality Gritstone was extracted in the 18th century. On the right, you pass by a lovely old house named Strawberry Gardens. This house was originally known as Lantie Gardens, after its builder. In Edwardian times, it was renowned as a local tearoom, and the delights offered could be enjoyed either inside or outdoors.

Fresh fruit such as cherries and gooseberries were sold from the orchard, and it is recorded that the owners occasionally supplied the Whitsuntide teas for the local Sunday school. The 1901 census records William and Mary Wilkinson living there, 66 and 70 years old respectively, and describes them as market gardeners.

From here you carry on down the well-used footpath between Hazel Head Wood and Willy Wood and walk on for a short while until you reach Tong Park war memorial where you could perhaps take a well-deserved breather.

This memorial commemorates the residents of Tong Park who were killed or missing in World War I (19 names) and World War II (2 names). It was erected in 1922-3 and was paid for by the Denby family who first came to Baildon in 1853 when William Denby Junior bought Gill Mill. It is situated in a rather strange but quaint position out in the countryside overlooking the Cricket pitch of Tong Park and the mill pond of the Worsted spinning and carding mill.

Gill Mill was built in 1778 and was the first steam-powered mill in the Bradford area by some eight years. A small steam engine was installed by Haliday and Watson in 1790 to add to the power already produced by the water from the adjacent millpond. The Cricket pitch sits in a natural amphitheatre, which in 1914 held a crowd of 3,000 spectators for a cup tie against Windhill. Tong Park Cricket Club was formed in 1880 and this is their third ground.

After your short rest at the War Memorial you continue on along Lonk House Road and over the railway tunnel to pause briefly at an outstanding row of former mill workers cottages named Primrose Row. Constructed of solid Sandstone blocks these cottages are fairly representative of the type of humble dwellings found all over the Bradford area in the vicinity of the many long since disappeared Victorian mills. From here it is only a short walk downhill to Otley Road and from there on into Shipley where you can catch any number of buses to return to Bradford to conclude this walk.

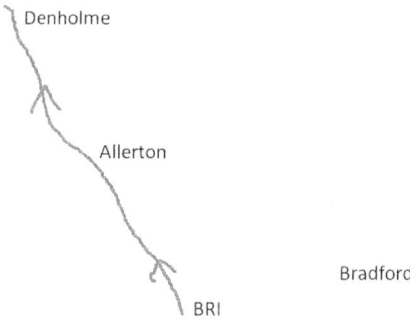

This particular walk begins at Bradford Royal Infirmary on Duckworth Lane. To reach here you can catch buses 615 or 618 from Bradford Interchange. The approximate distance for this walk is 4.0 miles.

The city of Bradford's main Hospital replaced the aged Victorian Infirmary on the end of Lumb Lane at Westgate in 1936. Bradford's Lord Mayor in 1908-09 Sir James Hill (11 March 1849 – 17 January 1936) devoted his year in office to raising £100,000 towards the cost of a new infirmary. He himself donated £30,000 but sadly died four months before the new Royal Infirmary on Duckworth Lane was opened. The final cost was £500,000 which was raised by public subscription, and this figure would equate to eighteen million pounds in today's money.

Situated directly across the road from the hospital is the magnificent Gothic entrance arch and lodge of Lady Royd Hall. This brooding Grade II listed Gothic house was designed by Bradford architects Milnes and Francis for the textile magnate Henry Williamson.

Constructed in close-grained Sandstone in 1865, it was a fine example of a mid-Victorian detached house displaying high levels of craftsmanship throughout.

The house retains much of its original layout including door cases with decorative mouldings, panelled doors, elegantly moulded plasterwork to ceilings and cornices in all the principal rooms together with many unique and detailed fireplaces throughout. It sits in an elevated position amidst mature and secluded north-south sloping grounds. In 1929, it was purchased by Bradford Girls Grammar school and has been in their hands until recently when it was offered for sale and redevelopment.

The gate lodge was constructed in the same style as were the further outbuildings, cottages, and stables connected with the house. During the Second World War, the house was used as both an evacuation and reception centre for girls from the south of England.

Following the perimeter wall of the grounds along Duckworth Lane you pass the coach house and stables as you make your way towards Allerton. After the junction with Crows Trees Lane, Duckworth Lane becomes Pearson Lane and this section of road is lined by a number of magnificent and imposing grand Victorian houses. These houses would have been built for fairly wealthy middle-class wool and textile merchants and perhaps the odd Bradford Solicitor or Doctor. Just a short way up Chellow Terrace to your right is a simple and plain Bungalow. Your attention is drawn to a most unusual large ornate sandstone arch guarding the driveway.

Quite obviously this was once the entrance to a much grander house than a mere bungalow, and this house was named Throstle Nest. Originally the site contained a small farmstead which belonged to a clothier named Richard Tetley, but this was replaced by the smart large Victorian house and attached gardens of Throstle Nest. This was built by a JP from Allerton named James Hill sometime in the 18th century.

Retrace your steps back to Pearson Lane before once again making your way towards Allerton. After passing by the old Prospect Worsted Mill on your right you arrived at Allerton's war memorial in Ladyhill Park. This stands in a nice peaceful little park directly opposite from the Prospect Methodist Chapel. The graveyard for the chapel contains eleven headstones that commemorate Commonwealth war graves.

Most of the remaining headstones are simply propped up against the perimeter wall that surrounds the graveyard. Leaving the graveyard behind you make your way down Chapel lane and turn right onto Grange Road. After passing the cottages that remain near the site of Allerton Grange on the left, you walk along Saffron Drive in the direction of Allerton Lanes. Keep going in a straight line and you will soon reach Allerton Lane. Turn left here and continue to walk for two hundred yards. Here, on your right, the former Allerton Parish Workhouse named Dean House comes into view.

Set slightly back from the road this house was built in 1605 by a Yeoman named Robert Dean. It was constructed in the "Halifax" style of coursed Sandstone and Gritstone, with a triple gabled front and mullioned and transom windows. The cornerstone panel on the left-hand gable is inscribed with the initials "RD" with a cross of The Knights of Jerusalem. Today it is a private residence of some interest in the local area.

Leaving behind Dean House, you now walk back up Allerton lane towards Hill Top and after passing by the site of the former Old Kings Head pub turn onto Cote Lane. After walking past a clutch of quaint old 18th century former Weavers cottages it is obvious that you have left the urban sprawl of Allerton behind and were starting to hit the countryside. The only house of any note on this stretch of country road is Smithfield House on the right opposite Moorhouse Moor.

This open moorland is dotted with old disused coal shafts and bell pits including the once quite substantial Allerton and Wilsden Colliery. The road here has no pavement and you have to be vigilant as the traffic passes by at speed as it always seems to do on open stretches of road like this. From this point the village of Wilsden can be seen far away in the distance to your right.

Continue along this road in a linear fashion for another mile before you reach the junction with Dean lane. Directly across from this point stood a Beerhouse named The Duke of York. Fifty yards before the junction you pass by the lane leading to a farm dated 1840 named The Mustard Pot. This Grade II listed building built of Sandstone with square mullioned windows has the most wonderful of names.

At the junction you turn left down Dean Lane towards the small row of former quarry workers cottages called Egypt. Apparently named to commemorate the invasion of Egypt by Napoleon in 1798 but in these parts you never know. The fields beside Dean Lane are pockmarked with the familiar scars and bumps of ancient quarrying activity and this is clear to see as you wind your way down the hill towards Egypt.

Stone was generally used for domestic building in the Bradford area from the mid-seventeenth century. By the eighteenth century, quarry and masonry methods improved and landowners' accounts indicate much rebuilding in stone and the opening up of delphs for wall stones. From the 1790s until the early nineteenth-century numerous active delphs were providing stone for enclosure walls, mills, and housing.

The early quarries at Bell Dean and Egypt probably opened to meet this growing demand. In 1876, there were thirty active quarries in the Egypt area employing four hundred and fifty workers some as young as eight years old. From 1860, the stone industry in Bradford boomed giving rise to investment in steam-powered machinery for lifting, transporting and sawing the stone. The double-sided row of cottages at the bottom of the hill was originally built to house workers and their family's from the nearby quarries There was a small Methodist Chapel to the rear but this closed in the 1960s. A local man named Arthur Jowett was the secretary of the Chapel for some forty-five years till it closed.

The road past the cottages was, until quite recently, enclosed by massive forbidding high stone walls known locally as "The Walls of Jericho". These were constructed to hold back the massive amounts of spoil which had been hewn from the ground over time in the pursuit of valuable stone. The walls are now gone and the road has been rearranged but one huge side piece right next to the end cottage survives. Perhaps if you rest a while here could almost hear the chip chip chipping sound of the men toiling in days gone by.

From this point you start up the steep winding Egypt Road towards The Rock and Heifer Inn. Notice the row of cottages built by quarry owner Jonathan Ackroyd on the junction. A date stone on one of the cottages indicates the date of construction as 1820. With the pub on your right you now climb gently up Rock Lane past another clutch of well preserved and loved quarry workers cottages at Back Heights. Small disused quarries were all around us as we approached another tiny hamlet named Moscow.

It is at this point that you turn right off the main road and headed down Ten Yards Lane. You are now heading for Doe Park Reservoir and then further beyond to your final destination of Denholme.

Passing the ancient and delectable Spring Hall Farm to your left, you soon come upon an oval shaped track in a field to your right. It is an oval track with short stout fencing on both the inside and the outside. It looked too small for the racing or trotting of horses or ponies.

The owner races Greyhounds all over the north of England and he uses it for himself and his friends to train and exercise their skinny and willowy hounds. From this point continue down Ten yards Lane for a short while and after passing a large quarry on the left you turn down a track at the end of the quarry. Continue down the thin rocky track towards the large body of water before you.

Doe Park Reservoir is a mid-size body of water situated to the east of Denholme village. It is surrounded by farmland on three sides and there is small sewage works between it and Denholme. It is quite an open reservoir with only a few small trees and shrubs to obscure the shoreline. It is higher up the same valley as Hewenden Reservoir and its river outlet eventually becomes Harden Beck.

The reservoir is fed by Stubden Beck which flows East down from the Stubden and Thornton Moor Reservoirs with Denholme Beck flowing North down Denholme Clough. There is also a sailing club and a small group of fishermen that use it on a regular basis. Activities on the water include sailing, canoeing, kayaking, dragon boating and raft building. It is also popular with bird watchers. Here birds such as Water Rail, Reed Warbler, Grasshopper Warbler and Pied Flycatcher have been seen among good numbers of common migrants. The Sewage works along the west side attracts Wagtails and Pipits on the filter beds as well as Finches and Warblers in the bushes surrounding them.

Walk across the concrete concourse at the head of the reservoir in the direction of your final destination in the village of Denholme. At the end of the concourse stands Reservoir House which is dated 1858. It is an impressive three bedroomed detached property located directly next to the Reservoir and surrounded by stunning rural views. It even has a gym apparently. From here you walk steadily up Foster Park View towards Denholme where you can catch bus number 67 back to Bradford to conclude this particular walk.

Bradford

Tong Street

Oakenshaw

Birkenshaw

Wyke

This walk commences at the end of Tong Street close to the famed Lapwater Hall. To reach here you can take a number of buses from Bradford interchange (620,256,425) the approximate distance for this walk is 4.60 miles.

Tong Street itself is a long and straight road and it should come as no surprise that it was once the main Roman road through this area. Many Roman artefacts such as coins and pieces of vases have been found over the years in this area, and there was even a Roman fort at nearby Hunsworth. But such ideas will be far from your mind as you leave the bus by the site of the long-gone Newmarket Colliery on Tong Street.

Today this area is simply a large field with only the odd bump and scrape on the ground to signify to its past use. It was for a time in the 18th century one of this area's many small coal pits and mines.

On the 11th of November 1854, there was a massive explosion caused by a build-up of Methane gas that took the lives of six local miners. Amongst those killed were William Blackburn, John Chadwick, John Runder and Peter Palmer.

After crossing Tong Street you walk down the side of the former pub, The Old Duke William and make your way down Cross Street towards part of Tong Moor and the site of the former Birkenshaw and Tong Railway Station.

This station which opened on the 20th August 1856, was on the Gildersome branch of The Leeds and Halifax Railway. It closed to passengers on the 5th of October 1953. Today the site is occupied by small light industrial units and no trace of the station remains.

After this point, Cross Lane becomes Station Lane as you walk past a series of substantial late 18th-century Victorian detached houses. Some of these were indeed rather grand and will have been built for high middle-class wool and textile merchants based in the city of Bradford or perhaps even Leeds. The road is lined with mature elderly trees and the high solid stone walls that usually denote the presence of houses of this nature. One of these houses, the grand Wynberg was designed and built around the turn of the 19th century and contains many of the fine architectural features of that period.

The house is soundly constructed of coursed stone under a multi-pitched slate roof. The generous family accommodation is arranged over 3 floors and includes two generous reception rooms, kitchen and utility arrangements, and six bedrooms and the house bathroom. After a few seconds of admiration of such a fine residence you can continue on down the leafy road towards the more working-class village of Birkenshaw.

Up to the 18th century, Birkenshaw was no more than a rural hamlet with a scattering of humble yet functional small cottages. The development of the village came with the purchase of land by the Emmet family and the establishment of a foundry for iron smelting. Although this foundry closed in 1815 the community was already well established and growing with the addition of work in local coal pits and the Woollen mills nearby.

The Emmet family made provision by granting, in 1828, land for the building of a church in the village. Parliament granted £3000 and the mock Gothic church of St Pauls was the result. The first Vicar died after only three months but his successor, Rev Henry John Smith, was vicar from 1832-1862. His contribution to the parish was outstanding. He began the Sunday school and then built two school buildings in the church grounds.

Crossing over the main Bradford Road, you enter a small area of tiny but still loved cottages called Furnace Lane. Walking beyond this you enter onto open countryside close to what is known as Navigation Bank. In 1780-1 John Emmet the Elder, Thomas Holden, William Bolland and William Emmet, iron founders of Halifax, leased land in Birkenshaw for a furnace and foundry, which was operating by 1782. Thomas Holden and William Bolland both withdrew their capital, leaving the company in difficulties and when the prices of iron goods slumped in 1815 the business closed.

Navigation Bank runs southwards from the foundry site. Little is known about it but there are three theories: that it was a canal to bring in supplies of coal and limestone, or to take away slag (to the 'blue hills', which might have been slag heaps), or that it was a linear reservoir to supply water for the water-wheel on Birkenshaw Beck. It was a strip of water retained by a bank constructed along the hillside, its inner wall faced with stone. Although it could have served as a catchwater drain, one would expect it to have had a fall towards the Foundry mill if that was its sole purpose.

You follow the bank for a short while then after a short while stumbling through the fields and over more than a few fences, you should see Lodge Beck and head for the dense woodland that surrounds the beck

Here the beck assumes a grotto-like appearance where ochre red coloured water runs down through a series of rough stone steps before disappearing away down through the vegetation. A wire fence is but a few feet away up the banking and with some effort you cross the beck and climb the bank.

Make your way across the field and head for Hunsworth Lane and eventually you will stubbled from the field onto the lane.

After a short march up Hunsworth Lane you reach Hunsworth Lower Lane and the farmhouse of Lower Copley. Here you will see a good old farmyard with all manner of vehicles and assorted equipment.

Sometimes in places like this you can see very old and ancient ploughs and the like but in one corner of this farmyard there are a number of battered and well used military vehicles. A rather strange sight in a West Yorkshire rural farmyard without a doubt.

After battling through more long grass fields, across Cockleshaw Beck and through the rather dense Chatts Wood you emerged on Cliff Holmes Lane near to the old Oak Mills at Oakenshaw. Originally a corn mill, Oak Mills was converted to textile use at the beginning of this century. It was previously a multi-storey stone-built structure which was damaged by fire many years ago.

Today only a small single-storey former stable building section remains. Now you are entering suburbia and civilisation as you pass through the roadway tunnel under the M606 Motorway and onto Wyke Lane.

A short walk up Wyke Lane brings you to The Oakenshaw Memorial Cross. This fine structure stands right in the middle of the road and traffic has to drive around the side of it to pass by. This large ornamental cross on a base of four steps was erected by the Lord of the Manor Dr Richard Richardson in 1702 in memory of his wife Sarah.

Erected on the site of a previous medieval cross, this Grade II listed slender stone column sits on a four-step circular podium. It is surmounted by an elaborate finial which has a sundial on each face. In the wall opposite is a stone carving containing the "Arms of Bradford" and the legend "Labor Omnia Vincit". It belongs to Cross House Farm, which was built in 1601.

Apparently it was brought here from the Bradford slaughterhouse in Hammerton Street by a previous owner who had a shop and wholesale business there. There is a similar one from the same source outside Cliff Hollins Farm nearby.

The section of Wyke Lane between The Memorial Cross and the disused Oakenshaw Railway tunnel further along contains a varied selection of 18th-century former quarry workers and weavers cottages. There is even a couple of the delectable one storey whitewash walled stone slate-roofed cottages known as "Low Deckers".

These can be seen all over Bradford, mostly in places near to long-gone quarries as they were usually home to the workers.

Soon you will reach Oakenshaw railway tunnel. This tunnel was constructed in 1848 to enable the road from Oakenshaw to Wyke to pass over the Low Moor fork of The Spen Valley railway line. This line formed part of the Lancashire and Yorkshire railway, and for much of the way at the Low Moor end it followed the route of the river Spen.

In 2001, a stretch of the disused line was converted to a cycling and walking route named The Spen Valley Greenway by SUSTRANS. The tunnel was constructed using the "cut and cover" method with one end collapsing during the building work.

From here you continue on past the tunnel and along Wyke Lane through a stretch of open countryside interrupted only by the cottages of Pearson Fold on your left before reaching the site of the former Ben Ing pit on your right.

This pit only operated for a short period from 1896 to 1905. Amongst the various bumps and lumps in the now reclaimed grassland, you may notice a small handful of metal vents denoting the sites of the former coal shafts themselves. From here you turn off to your right along Wilson Road and cross over the path of a former mineral railway.

This narrow-gauge rail track was used to transport minerals to the furnaces and factories at Low Moor Chemical Works nearby but as of today has long since disappeared. A short section of the old Wilson Road still shows the original cobbled surface. This whole area is pockmarked with old brickworks and coal shafts providing evidence of its rich industrial past.

Wilson Road will take you past the site of the former Storr Hill brickworks by Clay Hill Drive and then onto Huddersfield road where you can catch the bus (687,268,363) back to Bradford Interchange to complete this walk.

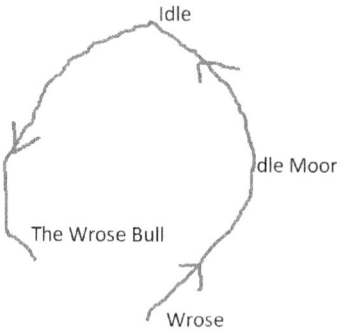

To ramble amongst the many ghosts of the past which surround this historical piece of Bradford you need to catch the 633 bus from Bradford Interchange. The approximate distance for this walk is 3.0 miles. The route of your walk takes you through land that still to this day shows evidence of long ago human industrial endeavour in the form of 18th-century coal pits and tiny Sandstone quarries. These are of course long gone but the evidence is there if you look for it.

You commence this walk on the Wrose Road end of Westfield Lane and soon you will be passing by cottages to your left that once belonged to Westfield Farm. Set back slightly from the road these quaint dwellings of simple rustic design are all that remain of a once busy and bustling farm.

Moving on you arrive at the junction with All Alone Road where the row of cottages named Starting Post are situated on the right. Constructed of coursed Sandstone bricks with a solid slate roof this short row of originally two cottages was built circa 1800. The third cottage was added at a later date as was the rear extension of the first two.

All Alone Road led originally to the first house to be built on the hillside overlooking Idle, right on the edge of the moor, and from the valley dwellers' point of view below, it must have looked "all alone" up on the hill.

But before that area is reached stop for a few moments at a point just by the present-day motor vehicle repair garage where what was known as the "Starting Stoup" used to stand.

The starting stoup, or post, was the area from which the Idle Moor Horse Races used to run from. In the Leeds Mercury of Tuesday 15th July 1729, and also on Tuesday 6th of July, 1731, it announces that: "races will be run on Idle over Moor by any horse, mare, or gelding for Plate of the value of £3 and £7." Today the area is covered by open fields which contain a handful of old stable buildings and horses belonging to the nearby Roleystone Horse and Pony Sanctuary.

It was also across this grassland that one of the few Second World War occurrences that involved the city of Bradford occurred.

The Battle of Britain was over and had been won by the RAF but the odd German Luftwaffe aircraft still roamed above the skies of Britain. On the night of 4th / 5th May 1941, a German Junkers Ju88 M2 twin-engine multirole aircraft was tasked with laying mines in the Irish Sea off Belfast. Over the North of England, they were intercepted by an RAF Bristol Beaufighter of 25 Squadron flown by P/O Kenneth Hollowell and Sgt Richard Crossman. One of the Ju88's engines was damaged over the Bradford area and after losing height and releasing the bombload, two of the crew bailed out.

The aircraft was attacked again which caused further damage and the two remaining crew left by parachute. The aircraft crashed into a wood yard and an adjoining row of houses centred on 13-15 High Street, Idle at around 00.45hrs. Sadly at least three civilians were unfortunately killed and four others injured with one succumbing to his injuries a few weeks later. One of the fatalities was a twelve-month-old baby girl.

The Luftwaffe airmen landed across the North-Leeds area; in the Guiseley, Otley, and the Farnley districts and were taken prisoner. The German pilot, one Ernst Jurgens drifted slowly down towards the fields close to the houses on Westfield lane. The pilot landed on Idle Hill near to what was Crockers Farm. According to reports two farmhands from All Alone Farm and other men ran to the field where the pilot was landing.

The German, apparently just happy to have survived the shooting down simply walked towards his captors with his hands in the air and surrendered.

The houses were never rebuilt and today the site of the crash on high Street has a simple seat with two raised flower beds marking it. There is a possibility that one of the engines remains buried at the crash site.

From this point you take the right-hand fork around the side of the garage and walk down the track next to what appears to be a graveyard of forklift trucks towards the former site of Israel Newton's Boiler Works on your left.

The firm of Newton and Sons took over this building and naming it Summerley Works, started to build and repair steam Locomotive boilers in 1906. Prior to this, the building was used as a stone sawing mill for the local quarries. The famous steeplejack and television personality Fred Dibnah MBE recorded a program in this building some time ago but today the site is empty. Newtons moved their business to Derbyshire some time ago and still do work for the heritage railways.

Carrying on you now head for the cottages of All Alone. Walking past the cluster of modern electric gated substantial houses that now adorn this part of All Alone Road, you turn left up a small track and soon arrive at the former farmstead. The house of All Alone farm was almost certainly built in the 18th century, though no records seem to survive of the actual date of its erection. Doctor Samuel Ellis came by the land on which the house stands in 1773, so it must have been built between then and 1777 when he had the land enclosed.

At All Alone Doctor Ellis cared for a single patient: the Hon. Luke Plunkett, son of the Earl of Fingall, Lord-Lieut. of Meath. It is unclear how this situation came about; it seems that the doctor was loath to leave his roots to travel to Ireland to attend the gentleman, and so perhaps the Irishman came here instead. Others who have lived here include the White family, of whose son, Mr. John White had his children taught by none other Charlotte Bronte. Over the years, the house has changed hands on many occasions, but the name of the building always remains unchanged – All Alone.

Turning around and leaving the cottages behind you walk towards Highfield Road and turn left to make your way down to the top of Idle village. Passing by the Yorkshire stone former Coach house of the long-gone grand Summerfield House on the left as you go. The 1901 census records one William Greenwood and his family living here.

Walking along Highfield Road you could admire the substantial late Victorian houses Briarfield, Barkhill House, Highfield View and Highfield House to your left.

All will have been built for wealthy and successful middle-class Victorians and their families and their presence still lends an air of refinement to the area.

From here you continue along Highfield Road till you reach Towngate. Here, opposite the White Bear public house, stands what is known as the Chapel of Ease. This Grade II listed building dates from 1630 and is currently occupied by the performing arts company of Stage 84. Consecrated in 1692, this course Gritstone stone slate-roofed building replaced an earlier chapel. Sometimes called the "Old Bell Chapel" after the first Minister Mr Bell it also housed the village lock-up. Turn left here along Westfield Lane which will take you up to Idle Hill and Catstones Wood.

Westfield Lane is flanked on either side by numerous marvellous 18th-century former weavers and quarry workers cottages, some of them listed buildings. After a short while you reach the ground of Hepworth and Idle Cricket Club. This quaint little village ground is built on the site of what was once Town End Quarry and behind the clubhouse stands the last of the three ventilation stacks for the sewage tunnel running from Frizinghall to Esholt.

Directly opposite the cricket ground is one of the most unusual and perhaps the smallest burial site you will come across on your travels. The ground for this ancient Quaker burial ground was donated by Joshua Bartlett, a prosperous Bradford bookseller, and a noted Quaker himself. Trustees for the plot of land were appointed and for a time, a Samuel Drake guarded the spot. Others followed, including Jeremy Grimshaw, Thomas Yewdall, and Benjamin Sandall. The first burials were Jeremiah Yewdall in 1690, son of Thomas (named above) and Benjamin Swaine. The last was his Great Grandson David in 1825. The name "Yewdall" appears on an original memorial stone that has been preserved and set into the ground.

The final body count was 30 I believe. You can enter the tiny square walled area by the Grade II listed archway facing onto Westfield Lane. As with all Quaker graves, the headstones are laid flat within. Local folklore says that a ghost can be summoned by running around the top of the flat top of the walls seven times "faster than is humanly possible" although this is to be taken with a pinch of salt.

Carrying on along Westfield Lane past the imaginatively named Carcase End farmhouse on High Busy Lane, you will soon reach the turn off to Low Ash Road on your right. This is more of a track than a road and will take you between Catstones Wood and Idle Hill up to Wrose Road.

As you arrive at the turn off glance around and notice the trademark undulating surface of a former quarry in the field opposite. Although the quarry had been filled in when it was abandoned many years ago the ground had settled over the subsequent years and has left quite a sizable dip.

This must have been one of the largest quarries in this area as its remains are larger than most. Over the road just along Westfield Lane is Roleystone Horse and Pony Sanctuary on the right. The resident horses have nowhere else to go and it really is the last chance saloon for most of them. A most noble venture

As you walk along the track towards Wrose you will be almost on top of one of the best spots in the area for sitting, thinking and peaceful reflection. So make a short detour through a fence on the right-hand side to perch yourself on a large flat piece of rock on Idle Hill looking down across the magnificent vista before you towards Baildon.

From here Charlestown can be seen and even the top of Hollings Hill at Guiseley. Esholt and its awesome woods can be seen in the distance to your right, whilst to the other side your eyes may pick out Saltaire and even the faint outline of Milner Field at Gilstead. It may be playtime at the junior school down at the bottom of the hill in front of you and perhaps you can hear the excited playful screams of innocent young children.

When you are done feasting your eyes return to the track above and continue to make your way towards ancient Catstones Wood. Coins and broaches from the First and Second centuries have been found in the vicinity at a nearby quarry. A Quernstone used for milling grain and corn was found was also found here in 1926. Even Roman coins were unearthed just over the track at the top of Idle Hill where the service reservoir now sits. Continue to walk along the track and you soon reach the site of an old maggot farm and a former Piggery to your left. The Piggery itself has been replaced by a smart detached house that continues to use the name "The Piggery".

You soon reach a small row of 18th-century cottages that is situated almost at the foot of the upper part of Idle Hill. The cottages are backed by a massive stone wall that was built to keep the hill from sliding down and crushing them. Across the track from here land slopes away quite dramatically to the right giving way to a plantation that is thick with mature trees and dense vegetation.

After passing cottages named Miserable corner you carry on past the house of Low Ash and the quite superb aged Wrose Brow Plantation falling away to your right. This place appears somewhat dark and brooding with almost a mystical feeling emitting from it, even in daylight.

On the far side of here is the site of the former Wrose Brow Brickworks. This concern was created for the manufacture of bricks and sanitary tubes to be used in local buildings. Ganister and pipe-clay was mined from the hillside and Wrose Hill bricks are common in Shipley and North Bradford. In the years 1901-1927 the company owning the works was known as Wrose Hill Fire Clay. A 1945 list of mines suggests that Wrose Hill was closed in July 1944. Today only the Manager's house, built in 1912 and named The Ridge survives.

As you continue to walk along the track you almost back in the centre of modern-day Wrose. The Bold Privateer comes into view at the end of Low Ash Road. This public house built in 1957 was named after The Earl of Cumberland who at one time owned all the land in the Wrose area at the time of Queen Elizabeth 1. We turned right here and walked along Wrose Road past the site of the demolished Catholic church of Our Lady and St. Anthony on your right. This was demolished in 1995 and replaced by sheltered housing bungalows. The Italianate style Presbytery beside it remains today as a private dwelling.

Your walk today ends at the superb Georgian style house that is the Wrose Bull public house. This building was formally the residence of Dawson Jowett, a well-respected local man who was the Master of The Airedale Beagles which were once kennelled here. The Airedale Beagles were established in 1891 through the co-operation of business and working men. This followed a chance encounter on Ilkley Moor between Dawson Jowett and Tom Clark. Tom became the kennel man and Dawson the huntsman. The Hunt had links to the Bradford Harriers that had disbanded just a couple of years before, and there was a long tradition of Beagling in the Jowett family.

The pub was originally named the Hare and Hounds but was nicknamed The Bull after a bull that was kept in an adjoining field.

Behind The Wrose Bull is the site of the "Wrose Elm". Once a focal point for the whole village it succumbed to Dutch elm disease in 2000 and was replaced with an Ash tree. Seeing as you are right next to one of the best watering holes in the area you could decide it is the right time to end your walk and call in for a pint. When you are suitably refreshed you can catch bus 633 from outside the pub to return to Bradford Interchange and conclude this walk.

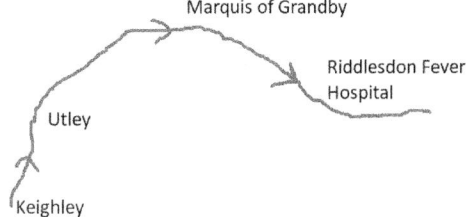

This historical walk begins in Keighley and the town can be reached from Bradford by taking the 662 bus from Bradford Interchange. The approximate distance for this walk is 4.0 miles.

Upon arriving at Keighley bus station you have to make your way along North Street and make for the general direction of an outlying village named Low Utley. North Street itself becomes Skipton Road and before long it leads you past Keighley's small rather worn out looking cinema and past a series of grand, substantial late Victorian terrace houses,

After a short stroll you arrive at the Gothic Revival entrance arch of Cliffe Castle. As is common with buildings of this age the sandstone is discoloured with age and fumes from the passing heavy traffic. Cliffe Hall was built by Christopher Netherwood between 1828 and 1833 and designed by George Webster of Kendal, a Gothic Revivalist. The Butterfields, a textile manufacturing family, bought Cliffe Hall in 1848. Henry Isaac Butterfield transformed the building by adding towers, a ballroom and conservatories from 1875 to 1880, and renamed it Cliffe Castle in 1878.

He decorated the building with the Griffin motif, which he had adopted as a heraldic crest. His Son Frederick inherited it in 1910 but allowed it to fall into disrepair.

In 1949, the building and grounds were bought by Keighley Corporation with the assistance of Sir Bracewell Smith, a local benefactor, who in 1955, paid for the conversion of the house for public use. The house had been gabled in the neo-gothic style, with tall towers at each end, and with added conservatories. In the interests of modernisation, the back tower was taken down, and the front one shortened. The high Flemish gables and other decorations were removed from the roof.

At the roundabout at the edge of the Cliffe Castle grounds the road becomes Skipton Road and continues along past a number of sturdy and well designed detached houses. These houses will have originally been constructed away from the late Victorian squalor and grime of Keighley town centre for local businessmen of some position.

At this point you are now just over a mile away from Keighley and approaching High Utley and the Victorian masterpiece that is Utley or Keighley Cemetery. As with most places of burial of this age it emits a feeling of brooding yet at the same time is tinged with one of peacefulness.

Opened in 1857 it now contains 57 Commonwealth War graves as well as the usual array of resting places of the local dignitary's long deceased. One particular interesting resident is Christopher Ingham who served in The Duke of Wellingtons 95th Rifle Regiment. He fought in ten battles against the French in Spain, France, and Belgium and even at the famous Battle of Waterloo. After being awarded The Peninsular Medal he died in 1866 and was buried with full military honours. The Television character "Sharpe" featuring Sean Bean is reputedly based on him. The things this man will have seen and done defy description and are difficult to comprehend.

The village of Utley itself is listed in 1086 in the Craven section of the Domesday Book as owned by the Viking Vilts. He was taxed on about 120 acres of arable ploughland here. He also owned Newsholme but shared Oakworth with Gamel Bern. It has been suggested that the name means oat field or outfield (of Keighley) or that it was a meadow (Ley) owned by Utta.

A short jaunty walk past the cemetery brings you to Birchwood Road on your right and you turn down here and pass by the smallest fish and chip shop you are ever likely to see. It is a tiny one pan operation no more than the size of a garden shed, but having said that this kind of places often serves up a far more appealing simple meal than the much larger concerns. From this point take Keelham Lane and carry on down towards the hamlet of Low Utley and from there across the River Aire and onto Keighley Golf Club.

The hamlet of Low Utley has the appearance of a time bubble. A tiny collection of mostly early 18th century humble workers cottages of simple design congregate around the lower end of Keelham Lane, it really is a case of stepping back in time. Almost every building is resplendent with aged mullioned windows, sandstone slate roofs, and tiny cottage gardens.

Grizzled and knarled toothless old women hang their washing out to dry in the warm sun as you stumble along the cobbles intoxicated with the history of these humble dwellings. This walk is worth it just to amble within this place and everything else is a bonus.

You exit the time capsule and cross over the railway bridge then over the modern A629 bypass before continuing along Parkers Lane to cross the River Aire by a metal road bridge.

Up ahead in the middle distance far beyond the golf course you can see the dense trees of Low Wood. Beyond here the Leeds and Liverpool Canal winds its relentest way through the countryside on its way towards the basin in Leeds.

Here you press on towards the canal and Booths Bridge. This small modern bridge over the canal was originally built of timber and is operated manually by a pivot on the north side. Look for a small traditional Lime Kiln in this area. It is situated down a bank at the side of the canal bridge on the south bank and is accessed by a rough rocky footpath that runs off the towpath.

Probably built after the canal was opened it is constructed of rubble stone with an arched opening leading to an arched roof space which contained the opening for the flue. Today it is in poor condition with trees growing out of the roof.

The common feature of early kilns was an egg-cup shaped burning chamber, with an air inlet at the base known as "the eye". Limestone was crushed (often by hand) to fairly uniform 20-60 mm lumps. Successive dome-shaped layers of limestone and coal were built up in the kiln on grate bars across the eye. When loading was complete, the kiln was kindled at the bottom, and the fire gradually spread upwards through the charge.

When burnt through, the lime was cooled and raked out through the base. Fine ash dropped out and was rejected with the "riddlings". Typically the kiln took a day to load, three days to fire, two days to cool and a day to unload, so a one-week turnaround was normal. Such kilns were constructed near to the canal for the easy method of transportation of the raw materials and the quicklime that was produced.

Quicklime was used as fertilizer and in mortar for constructing buildings. The development of the national rail network increasingly made the local small-scale kilns unprofitable, and they gradually died out through the 19th century. They were replaced by larger industrial plants. At the same time, new uses for lime in the chemical, steel and sugar industries led to large-scale plants. These also saw the development of more efficient kilns.

From Booths Bridge you continue along the path through Low Wood and a number of Sandstone escarpments that make up Carr Delph and onwards in the direction of Riddlesden. The area to your left is riddled with tiny ancient coal pits dotted amongst the dense woodland.

The path stayed near to the canal bank and you may notice some coped moorings that indicate that stone was taken from the quarry directly onto the canal boats for transportation elsewhere. Walking along the well-trodden trail through the woodland on the edge of Carr Delph you trek up through the smaller Riddlesden Golf Course on a section that was surprisingly cobbled like the tiny street in Low Utley.

You will now have reached Clough Beck where the area is also littered with more small coal pits. Now long gone and forgotten there is little evidence of their industrial past. The previously dense woodland thins out around the beck and you follow the beck uphill towards the Bradford Corporation Water Works Barden Aqueduct. This still forms part of the system that brings water to the city of Bradford from far away reservoirs on the moors above. The steady flow of the beck runs over a series of rocks at this point forming a small waterfall.

Here you move through the trees, over a high drystone wall and set off in the direction of Dunkirk Wood. Continue along the track through the fields, past rundown and ramshackle humble homes of horses until you reach a small wood. From there you walk downhill past the vegetation ridden site of a long-forgotten small Sandstone delph till until you reach a small row of terraced cottages called High Cote.

Sat above the canal bank this terrace of stone-built cottages occupies an elevated position at the top of a steep wooded bank. Built in the first half of the 19th century of coursed local stone with solid slate roofs these cottages sit in an area of some tranquillity. Following on along the small road alongside the cottages you now reach Leach's Bridge and before long arrive at West Riddlesden Hall.

Considered to be of national interest, this fine example of a 17th century Manor House stands in well-wooded grounds. The Grade I listed building was the longtime residence of the Maud family before being passed to the Leach family in the 17th century. Constructed of hammer-dressed stone with a stone slate roof it has a south-facing front dominated by three gabled bays. The central doorway includes a torus-moulded architrave on plinth blocks. A date stone of 1687 with the initials TL (Thomas Leach) adorns the front. In the Interior, there is an oak-panelled hall with dated beam and open-string staircase with turned balusters.

After pausing for a few moments to admire this fine old building you continue along Limekiln Road and skirt lower Morton Banks before arriving at Stockbridge Wharf. This is where the canal takes on an industrial feel due to the tall former warehouses alongside that have been converted into flats. The other side of the canal has houses with gardens that run right down to the water's edge. Although the warehouses still retain the original loading bays the lifting mechanisms have been removed. The wharf was originally built to allow the transportation of goods and materials to Keighley as it was not served by the Leeds and Liverpool canal.

We carried on walking on this side of the canal for a short distance until we reached Banks Bridge. This modern structure carries Granby Lane over the canal and has a stone-built overflow on the far side which is most unusual. Here you will find the famed and ancient Marquis of Granby public house.

This building is of considerable age and may have been constructed along with the canal. Constructed of dressed deep course stone with a stone slate roof, it has sadly lost some of its original character due to the replacement of multi-pane sash windows with more modern UPVC replacements. Next door to the pub is a quaint small single-bay shop built in 1880.

You are now on what is known as Hospital Road, and although today there is no Hospital here there once was many years ago. At one time in the past, there were many fever or isolation hospitals dotted all around the Bradford area, even one near to Top Withens on Haworth Moor. Before the discovery of Penicillin and the advent of modern health care the world was awash with many contagious diseases.

Most of these have now been eradicated or at least brought under some degree of control. Prior to that though it was a different scenario and deadly diseases such as Smallpox, Typhoid, Scarlet fever and Typhus were widely prevalent throughout the Western World. So to aid in the recovery from these type of diseases and to prevent the spread of infection many Isolation hospitals sprang up around this area.

Morton Banks Fever Hospital or The Keighley and Bingley Joint Isolation Hospital as it was also known as was one such place, and it was this establishment that once lay at the end of Hospital Road. Most if not all of these places are long gone but the old Ordnance Survey maps show them still.

The Keighley and Bingley Joint Isolation Hospital opened on "a most eligible site" at Morton Banks, in February, of 1897, and by the end of the year had treated 131 patients with infectious diseases, including two of the nurses, one of whom had contracted scarlet fever and the other typhoid fever. Another 240 were admitted in 1898, including 67 with diphtheria. That year a further smallpox hospital was built a little higher up the hillside.

Morton Banks had 746 beds and reportedly dealt with more than 13,000 sick or wounded military men, some of whom came from as far away as Canada and the Fiji islands. There were 114 deaths including 42 Germans in the wake of the great Influenza Epidemic at the end of World War I. The hospital was even visited by American Military surgeons studying developments in military surgery, and advances were made in the treatment of Tetanus, gas poisoning, and Gangrene. In 1938, there were 415 admissions, with diphtheria accounting for 286.

At this point you make your way towards the gated and walled entrance that is all that remains of this weird place. The hospital was a series of buildings and huts contained within a walled compound but a lot of this has now been built on with modern housing. The area that remains is heavily wooded by the passage of time but you can find some evidence of its former use inside this tree infested area.

You could be rambling around in any number of heavily wooded plantations. You could be in Esholt Woods or the ruins of Milner Field at Gilstead as there seems to be no sign of its former grisly use at first glance. But you possess the knowledge of what this place once was and that may give you a sense of respect so tread upon the ground carefully.

When inside the wooded area look for a series of red bricks laid in the ground which obviously denote part of the foundations of a building. Then you may see a large cut in the soil containing a protruding sewage pipe. As you walk along through the trees more evidence comes into view. Amidst large pieces of broken toilet pottery a whole series of drains and their associated pipework lay before you. If you have a vivid imagination and have the knowledge of what it all once was then you can build a picture and get a feeling.

Make your way through the wooded area and traverse the whole area before ending down at the southern wall next to the canal. How Beck runs down the other side of the copse and to leave this area you follow that back uphill to exit the site onto Saxilby Road, Then you simply walk through an estate of new build houses to join Swine lane and then walk down onto Bradford Road to wait for the 662 bus back to Shipley. From there you can catch any number of buses to take you back to Bradford interchange to complete this walk.

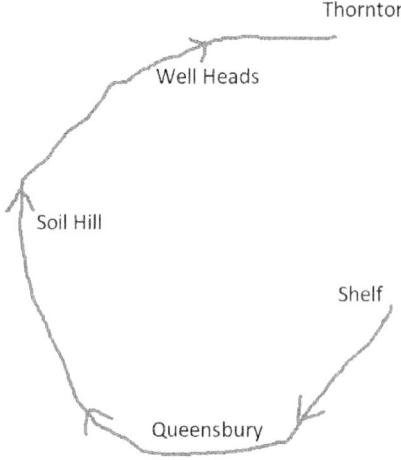

The starting point for this walk is the road formally known as The Shelf Foundry and Stone Tables Branch of the Leeds and Halifax Trust Toll Road, or Cooper Lane if you want to use the modern name. To reach this point at the Horton Bank end of cooper Lane you can catch buses number 681 or 571 from Bradford Interchange. The approximate distance for this walk is 5.80 miles.

Toll roads or Turnpikes such as this one, covered the whole area of not just Bradford but most of Wales as well. Turnpike trusts were established in England and Wales from about 1706 in response to the need for better roads than the few and poorly maintained tracks then available. Turnpike trusts were set up by individual Acts of Parliament, with powers to collect road tolls to repay loans for building, improving, and maintaining the principal roads in Britain.

At their peak, in the 1830s, over 1,000 trusts administered around 30,000 miles of turnpike road in England and Wales, taking tolls at almost 8,000 toll-gates. The trusts were ultimately responsible for the maintenance and improvement of most of the main roads in England and Wales, which were used to distribute agricultural and industrial goods economically.

The tolls were a source of revenue for road building and maintenance, paid for by road users and not from general taxation. The turnpike trusts were gradually abolished from the 1870s.

So after leaving the bus we started to walk down the slight gradient towards the main road which runs through Shelf village. It may be hard to believe that almost half of the length of Cooper Lane to your left was once covered by a large wood named Reevy Hall Plantation.

Upon reaching the same roundabout at the bottom, turn right along Carr House Road and walk for a short distance before reaching an old Independent Methodist Chapel named The Bethel Chapel. The whole area to the left of the roundabout was, a century ago, a veritable hive of fearsome industrial activity with many foundries and chemical works crammed into a square quarter-mile.

Built in only 139 days and opening in September 1853, this large sombre building enjoys a very large well-kept graveyard which contains the graves of some 4944 people. One most interesting grave contains the mortal remains of "the man who broke the bank at Monte Carlo".

Joseph Hobson Jagger was an engineer at Bottomley's Mill in Shelf and in the 1870s he went to Monte Carlo to visit the casinos. Using his engineering skills he studied the Roulette wheels and devised a method with which to beat it. On July 7th, 1875 he placed his first bet and eight days later he had won two million old French Francs. This would be the equivalent of £400,000 today which in the 1870s was a huge sum of money. His secret method to beat the system was all to do with the cylinders of the Roulette wheel apparently.

Leaving the Chapel graveyard, you continue along the main road for only a short time until you turn right up Burned Road. You will pass by the fine Upper Witchfield House, from where a tunnel was reputed to have run to the nearby Windmill.

This corn windmill was the last in the district to survive, and before falling into disrepair it remained as a local landmark until in 1960 when the top of the building was destroyed by a lightning strike before being finally demolished in 1964. Each of the four sails was seven feet in width and sixty feet in length and weighed one ton. In 1904, the sails were removed and a steam engine was introduced to provide power to grind the corn from the local farms. In 1914, the owner at the time Francis Barraclough closed the business and it remained unused until its final demise.

The actual site of the Windmill is now simply a piece of scrubland behind the remaining adjacent cottage on the left-hand bend of Burned Road. Standing there is it not difficult to use your imagination and conjure up visions of the massive lofty sails thundering through the air as they whirled through their repetitive windy dance. From this point you move on past some modern boring bungalows on Stanage Lane until the passing scenery develops a more countryside feel to it.

The grassy mounds to your left are the spoil heaps from long extinguished tiny coal pits. Climb a sizable grass-covered spoil heap on the right and you have a great view of an with a most unusual sight at the point where Stanage Lane becomes Bracken Lane.

Before you stands a large square stone gateway with a resting stone Lion perched upon the top. To each side is a smaller arched gateway but all three entrances will be locked. Not surprisingly this is known locally as The Lion Gate and once formed the Southern entrance to an estate known as Low House.

John Hirst bought Low House in 1665 which was then known as Brightwater. Yarn was spun for a while on handlooms on premises adjoining Low House. Sometime after that Joseph Hirst and Henry Sagar Hirst formed Low House Brewery and subsequently named it The Lion Brewery. Joseph died in 1890 and in 1893 his Sons sold the whole estate to Bentleys Breweries.

Moving off from the Lion Gate you soon pass by the location of the long-gone hamlet of Upper Bracken Beds. This stood at the far end of the next little track to your right. This was recorded as having being built in the 18th century possibly by Ayton and Elwell the bridge builders and founders, for their workers. Today only a small number of bumps and humps in the ground remain as evidence of this small hamlet.

Moving on along Brackens Lane you pass more former small coal pits and join Giles Hill Lane before passing by the 18th-century farmhouse named Green Head. By this point, the fields are open and expansive and the road is straight and true. In the middle distance you can see the farmstead and buildings of Long Lover and before long you will arrive at the main Brighouse Road.

You are now approaching the open expanses of the Queensbury area, and crossing over the Brighouse and Denholme Road you continue along Jackson Hill Lane. To the right is a terrace of four 18th century cottages preceded by a small row of those tiny dwellings known as "Low Deckers" These common one-room cottages are dotted all over the South Bradford area. They were rented by labourers who worked in the local mining and quarrying business.

Directly across the junction of Jackson Hill Lane and Paw Lane there was once a tiny two cottage hamlet named Paw. Nothing now remains apart from a scrape in the ground surrounded by a small earth bank. Again, those with a vivid imagination could be transported back to the time when these dwellings were home to perhaps a simple Quarryman or Miner and his small family.

What did they eat? How did they dress? Did they go to church in their Sunday best every week? Did they fear God or did the Father forsake his family and squander his wages on ale in the taverns of Queensbury?.

Turning right at the junction you continue down Syke Lane and very quickly pass by the 16th-century mullioned window farmhouse of Collier Syke before turning off up Deanstones Lane towards the site of a former fever hospital at Long Lane.

Built in 1893 in the days when infectious diseases were still a major problem, Long Lane Fever Hospital was a twenty-bed facility built by the local health board. Constructed on land bought from Geo Ambler for £280 the first ten years saw 251 patients admitted (249 for Scarlet Fever, 1 for Diphtheria and 1 for Enteric Fever). Since the discovery of Sulphonamides in 1937, Penicillin in 1929 and the subsequent inoculation program the hospital closed in 1945. Today the site is occupied by an estate of new build houses.

Continuing along Deanstones Lane you soon reach the West End part of the village of Queensbury. On the right at the junction, on the gable end of a row of three early 18th-century terrace houses are four large bricked-up former windows. They were bricked up to avoid the dreaded "Window Tax".

The window tax was a property tax based on the number of windows in a house. It was a significant social, cultural, and architectural force in England, France, and Scotland during the 18th and 19th centuries. To avoid the tax some houses from the period can be seen to have bricked-up window-spaces (ready to be glazed or reglazed at a later date).

In England and Wales, it was introduced in 1696 and was repealed in 1851, 156 years after first being introduced.

Here you turn left towards Halifax and walk for a short distance until turning right up Fleet Lane and at the precise spot of the second turning off to your left (Weston Avenue), you cross over the old railway tunnel that took the line from Staines cutting on to Queensbury Station. From here you pass by another short row of the lovely one decker workers cottages and a succession of larger local vernacular style cottages on Fleet Lane before stopping for a few moments to admire the coursed Sandstone detached cottage of Upper Fleet House.

Passing between Queensbury Park and the site of the former Mountain and Pineberry Quarry you join the Brighouse and Denholme Road again which would take you over towards the highest place in the Bradford area, Soil Hill.

Queensbury is known as the highest village in England and judging from the view from this point that title is well deserved. Glance over the drystone wall and you can clearly make out the far-away shape of Idle Hill in the distance. The massive chimney of Listers Mill in Manningham is also visible as is Salts Mill in faraway Saltaire. The view is simply stunning from here as the fields and countryside just seemed to open up down in front of you. Continued walking and before long you enter the small collection of former mill cottages and houses known as Mountain.

As the name suggests the area is as high as a mountain and provides a fantastic vantage point with which to overlook the whole city of Bradford. It is said that on a clear day no less than three of England's National Parks can be seen from here. The Peak District to the south, The Yorkshire Dales to the north and in the very far distance The Hambleton Hills on the edge of the North Yorkshire Moors.

A little further on along Brighouse and Denholme Road we came to The Raggalds Inn. Now renamed as "The Queen's Head" it is located in stunning surroundings and affords magnificent views across Calderdale. This infamous country pub, and restaurant has achieved a degree of notoriety due to a double shooting and a murder in 1995.

Original a staging post for the cloth trade at the end of the Industrial Revolution, the earliest record of its existence is in 1845. On the 24th April 1995, two masked men burst in and armed with a sawn-off shotgun and a pistol, shot dead the landlord Michael Briggs and wounded a customer. Two local men were later convicted and sentenced to life terms plus 15 years for the killing. It was said that the murder was carried out on behalf of rivals of Mr Briggs. Strangely enough, the name Raggald is a local term originating from Old Norse meaning villain or ruffian.

From the former Raggalds pub you continue on up Perseverance Road towards Soil Hill. If your visit is in spring then you may closely observe newly sheared Sheep as they lay sleeping in the warm early summer sun in the fields to your left. To your right the road is lined with humble sandstone former quarry workers cottages. You can clearly see Soil Hill now as it starts to rise up at the top of the road.

The object on this road that everyone notices is a monument stone that stands on the right side after two hundred yards. It commemorates the opening of the road in November 1871 as prior to that date the road was unmade and fully deserved its nickname of "Mucky loin"(lane). This road had long been problematic in winter as water from the moorland above caused rutting down past the row of cottages. At the bottom, the fields were often flooded, and hence the road too.

The residents of the adjacent houses and farms clubbed together to finance the construction (£75) of the road but it took so long that it was named "Perseverance" Road when it was finally completed.

The residents provided the labour themselves to save on the construction costs. Today the road appears quite civilised but its long straight rise does give you an indication of how tiresome it would have been to transverse in the days before the modern construction.

After passing the farmhouse of Small Tail and its adjacent roadside cottages, the road turns left and skirts along the side of Soil Hill. At 1300 feet above sea level Soil Hill or Swilling Hill (to use its ancient name) is the highest point in the Queensbury and surrounding area and naturally affords views that can only be dreamt about.

On this stretch of road are the properties of Sun Farm, Millers Row and Cloth Row or Hall as it is known today. Sun Farm was formally known as "Charnocks" after the family who occupied it in the seventeenth century. From the early eighteenth century to 1906 there was a Beer House at the farm. This was originally named The Gin Pit and latterly The (Rising) Sun. Its time of glory was perhaps in 1803 when it was chosen as a beacon site in case of invasion by Napoleon.

As you pass these properties you must be on the lookout for a track that leads off the road to the right, past a covered reservoir and up towards the summit of Soil Hill. Once you have traversed a cattle grid set in the track you will see one of the few complete Dew Ponds not just in this area but in any area.

The Dew Pond is only a few feet away to your left and, surrounded by its defence of small standing stones, it stands out in this somewhat barren landscape. The flat stones are arranged in such a way as to preclude larger beasts such as cattle from entering the pond and destroying the bottom layer therefore allowing the captured moisture to dissipate. Smaller animals like Sheep can access the water through the narrow entry point.

A Dew Pond is a small artificial body of water usually sited on the top of a hill which is intended for watering livestock. Dew ponds are used in areas where a natural supply of surface water may not be readily available. They are usually shallow, saucer-shaped and lined with puddled clay, chalk or marl on an insulating straw layer over a bottom layer of chalk or lime.

To deter earthworms from their natural tendency of burrowing upwards, which in a short while would make the clay lining porous, a layer of soot would be incorporated or lime mixed with the clay.

The clay is usually covered with straw to prevent cracking by the sun and a final layer of chalk rubble or broken stone to protect the lining from the hoofs of sheep or cattle. It is one of the few remaining Dew Ponds that remain in a complete condition with surrounding stones anywhere around these parts.

This area of Soil Hill is popular with bird watchers or "Twitchers" as they are known. The air will be still and silent and this only serves to enhance the feeling of isolation.

Between the sixteenth and nineteenth centuries, Soil hill was one of the busiest coal mining areas in the Halifax coal bed. The circular remains of the tops of the old pit shafts are still visible on its slopes. The coal was near to the surface and provided a ready supply to the local industries.

Another of Soil Hill's greatest virtues was the certain type of clay that laid underneath the soil and top turf along its summit. This substance was ideal for making pottery amongst other things and the last remaining Potter working from the Kilnworks down on the Ogden side was a man named Isaac Button. To reach this point you must slowly traverse down the Eastern side of Soil Hill directly beyond the Dew pond.

Built around 1900, this brick building with a Welsh slate roof runs east-west adjacent to east end at the top of the hill slope. Within the western part was a bottle kiln with internal radial walls and six segment- arched fire holes around the perimeter. Four flues from beneath the kiln floor run up the hill to the square chimney. Two of these heated the drying shed adjacent to the kiln and two heated a parallel pent-roofed shed where clay slurry was dried before forming. This method of firing and ventilation and the use of waste heat to dry slurry represent an important innovation in earthenware manufacture.

Issac Button was one of the last true English Country Potters and he was renowned for making a ton of clay pots in any 1 day. In fact, he was once timed from throwing the lump of clay onto the potter's wheel, producing an excellent pot and then cutting it off using a wire cutter which in total took him 22 seconds. This would translate into 120 pots in any one hour and up to 1200 in any one day.

By 1900 England had only around one hundred country potteries and sadly by the end of the depression no more than a dozen. At Soil Hill there had been a pottery facility since the 17th century and before the First World War this pottery shop employed thirteen men. As time passed, Mr Button ended up working the pottery business on his own because he could not find anyone to take an apprenticeship with him. He passed eighteen years working there on his own.

Now you need to get back to the track and continue to the summit where you can see down the far side of the hill. You can make out the cottages of Shay Bottom on the main road next to where a small narrow gauge railway used to run up into the quarry. We had to get across this open and busy landscape to continue on to Keelham and up to Wellheads in Thornton.

Look to the West and you can make out the former homes of the famous mill-owning Foster family of Denholme, Waterloo House and White Shaw, and the long straight road leading to Oxenhope, Long Causeway. Even Thornton Moor Reservoir is visible from your lofty seat. Now you must head for the main road and continue on to Keelham.

Turn right by the tiny school and the handful of former mill workers cottages in Keelham to take on the final short leg of this great walk. This is Well Heads which was formally known as Close head Lane and this road will take you onward towards the village of Thornton. It crosses over the railway tunnel by the cottages named "Well heads" and passes the upper section of Thornton cemetery on the right side. As you pass the White Horse Inn, look above the door for a date stone with the year 1815 carved into it.

Upon reaching the village of Thornton you can catch the 67 bus back into Bradford to complete this walk.

Bolton Woods to Northcliffe Park Shipley

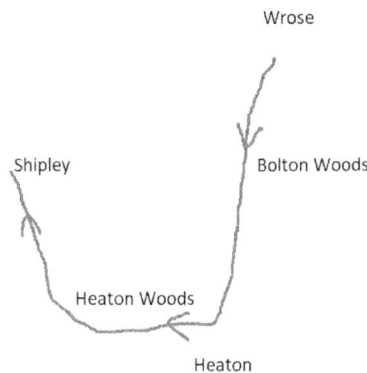

Wrose

Shipley

Bolton Woods

Heaton Woods

Heaton

This walk begins in the Swaine House area of North Bradford at the end of Wood Lane. To reach here you catch either bus 612 or bus 633 and get off near Hanson school. The approximate distance for this walk is 4.1 miles.

Wood Lane itself, after passing through a small council estate is no more than a mere footpath that leads around the side of Bolton Woods quarry and down towards Canal Road. But in days of yore, this track was part of the main trail from Idle Moor that the merchants and farmers would take when transporting their goods to the markets of Bradford.

Follow the well-worn path that skirts around the quarry and head down the hill. The Quarrymen appear to work one part of the quarry for a few weeks then move to another for a while. Although not as busy and industrious as in years gone by it is still worked on a limited scale to produce stone for small local projects. On occasion, the blasting of rock can be heard breaking the silence of the early morning, and the chipping of the Stonemasons tools ring out as they work the blocks of stone.

You are to walk down what is known as Hepolite Scar on the far side before making your way towards the old and historical settlement of Frizinghall. Hepolite Scar is the local name given the steep slope that rises up from Canal Road towards the top of the massive spoil heap of the quarry. Decades ago people would race their motorbikes up this slope in timed hill climbs and the name originates from a local factory that once made pistons and their rings for car and bike engines that were named "Hepolite".

The tiny long since disappeared hamlet of Delf Hill used to sit nearby but today the site is taken up by a small junior school. Pass through a small patch of moorland and make your way down onto the main road through the village of Bolton Woods.

Long established as a thriving industrial village due to its two mills, Bolton Woods is now a fairly quiet place where even the old blocks of council flats have now been demolished. Passing by the site of the also demolished Oswain Mill and over one of the remaining Bradford Canal bridges we were soon at the junction with Canal Road. Stop here for a few minutes to observe the gentle rush of Bradford Beck on your right as it weaves its way across its brick-lined bed to make its way to join the River Aire at Shipley.

Busy Canal Road is always a pain to cross but from there is it a short walk over the railway bridge and along Frizinghall Road towards the historical village of Frizinghall and one of the best pubs in the area, The Black Swan.

Situated next to a Grade II listed row of rendered Sandstone cottages, this mid to late 18th-century pub is a great place in which to enjoy some fine summer evenings. The oak beams and numerous horse brass's inside give it the feeling of a time capsule and the ale is not bad either. The adjacent row of cottages named Swan Hill is possibly the oldest part of Frizinghall having being built in the early part of the 18th century with numbers 2-7 being Grade II listed.

Passing by the sports grounds of Bradford Grammar School and a row of early 19th-century terrace houses you soon came to a small group of cottages on the left in an area known as Carr Syke. These are named after the beck which runs through nearby Lister Park, under the lake and waterfall and then under the Grammar school. The local Tollhouse was situated near here in 1816.

Lister Park is situated about a mile outside the city centre on Manningham Lane. It is one of the city's largest parks and was donated to the City of Bradford by Samuel Cunliffe Lister, who built Lister's Mill. The park has been successfully renovated in recent years, the lake has been re-opened for boats and a Mughal Water Garden constructed. There are also tennis and basketball courts, bowling greens and a children's playground. Lister Park contains the Cartwright Hall art gallery, where permanent and temporary exhibitions of modern and traditional art can be seen. But today you are not to visit Lister Park and instead you must make your way up Emm Lane, passing by the former Turf public house before heading towards Heaton.

According to contemporary reports, a previous landlord of The Turf, a Mr E Jowett shot and killed a rabid dog after it was seen "behaving in a strange condition". Part of this pub collapsed in 1894 during alteration work with the landlord and twelve other men being injured as they lay buried in the ruins under the scaffolding and fallen masonry. The two most badly injured men were an apprentice named Holroyd and a stonemason named Redmond. They were both dug out of the ruins still alive but in an unconscious state.

From here you continue up forbidding and steep Emm Lane heading past The University of Bradford School of Management and an assortment of fine late Victorian semi-detached and detached houses. Most of these houses are extremely grand and most have balconies and castellated turrets along with fine mature wooded grounds as befitting their status as dwellings of quite wealthy Bradfordians from the last century.

Many were built in the "Arts and Craft" style in the years 1880-1909. Yorkshire stone is most commonly used in brick form at ground level with a course render. In some examples, timber breaks up the render to give a mock Tudor effect. The windows and doors often incorporate attractive leaded and stained glass to great effect.

The wide leafy suburban road lined on each side with mature trees soon gives way to houses of a more humble nature as you approach the village of Heaton. The Yorkshire Ripper Peter Sutcliffe lived with his wife Sonia not far round the bend at 6 Garden Lane but you are not going that far and you must turn off down Quarry Street next to Heaton Cemetery.

This small and superb Victorian graveyard contains over 1100 graves and was instituted in 1824. It is the final resting place of several thousand paupers and children who were buried in communal graves of which there are no records.

From here you stroll down Quarry Street in a jaunty manner, past 18th-century cottages complete with the obligatory bricked up tax avoiding windows down towards Heaton Woods and the famous "Cat Steps". These steps were nicknamed so due to their step nature that "only a cat would choose to climb them"

Heaton Woods is an ancient woodland situated on a steep-sided gully and has been protected in recent years from any development. Today it is a valued local beauty spot where Deer still roam and Sparrow Hawks hunt the sky looking for prey below. At night Bats and Owls rule the quiet expanse of heavy, thick tree laden wood, and even the tops of the trees form a great canopy above you to block out the sunlight. A menacing and brooding feeling pervades the still air giving the wood an almost primaeval feeling.

Distant creatures can be heard scurrying amongst the undergrowth as you plod down the sloping gully towards the floor of the valley. As you weave your way down through the trees you may notice an old metal gatepost on the end of a fallen drystone wall. A gateway to where? There is no evidence of anything ever being here.

Continue along through the wooded area towards the sound of rushing water. Try to avoid falling headlong into Red Beck as you slide down the banking after snagging your leg on a large exposed tree root. The name of the beck was obviously a nod to the fact that the water that emanated from beneath the track beside was coloured with an orange-red tint. This is caused by the water running through natural Ironstone rock and is widely prevalent in many of the local streams and small becks in the Bradford area.

Continue on through Cliff Rods Wood and follow the route of the beck and within a couple of minutes you will be standing on a bank overlooking Shay Lane. This area of woodland is very dense with holly bushes alongside the ever-thickening stout trees and it may be hard work to traverse through such an environment. So when you came across a tiny ancient pathway you should follow this towards the distant sounds of golf balls being struck.

The familiar sound of passing traffic is almost upon you now as you surface onto Bingley Road. The road is long and straight as you pass by the site of a demolished cottage hospital before turning down High Bank Lane in the direction of Dungeon Wood.

The road on High Bank Lane contains no pavement on which to walk so you have to take care as the traffic speeds past. Looked over to your left and take in the quite magnificent view over towards Baildon Moor. Your final destination of Shipley sits at the foot of the valley below but is unseen from here. After a while a large expanse of grass opens up to the side of the road and you can walk on here until you reach North Cliffe Golf Club.

The information board at the entrance told me that it was a vast natural habitat for many varieties of wildlife and birds. The field leads you gently downhill towards North Cliffe Park and after passing by the pavilion and the Tennis Courts you emerge onto Bradford road by the main gates. Back in suburbia and civilisation, it is but a short distance through the side streets to the familiar bus stop outside the Weatherspoon's pub, The Sir Norman Rae where you can catch any number of buses to take you back to Bradford to complete this walk.

Thackley Corner to High Esholt

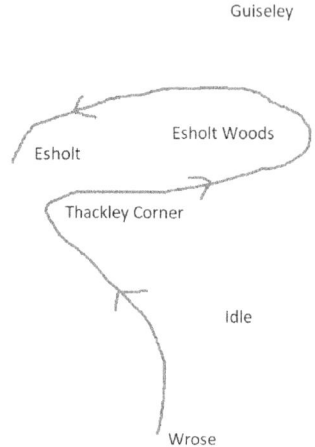

Guiseley

Esholt Woods

Esholt

Thackley Corner

Idle

Wrose

To reach the starting point for this walk you need to take the 612/613/633 bus from Bradford Interchange. The approximate distance for this walk is 3.0 miles.

At Thackley corner on the junction of Town Lane and Leeds Road stands an old open-air gents urinal. It is in the wall on the opposite side of the road from the sandwich shop and the barbers. A strange little place it is no more than a slit in the wall behind which stands a trough. It has not been used for decades officially but judging by the smell it continues to be used by blokes when they leave the nearby Great Northern pub I assume.

You need to walk down Thackley Road and using the road bridge you pass over the long-gone railway line of the Shipley branch of the Great Northern Railway. Carry on towards Ainsbury Avenue which winds down the edge of ancient Buck Woods to the canal. There is reputed to be a wartime bunker set in the banking along here where the Police would explode in safety any ordnance they came across.

Buck Wood is quiet and still as you plod downhill along the wide avenue. Only the distant birdcalls brake the silence as you pass by Field Wood and then Hollins Wood.

At this point, there is no mistaking that Esholt sewage works are nearby as even if the breeze blows downwards to hell it still pervades your nostrils like a fart in a sleeping bag.

But thankfully you are to cross the canal at the turn bridge and follow the towpath towards Apperley Bridge. It would be nice to go straight ahead through the sewage plant at the bridge but it's always locked up tight so there is no choice but to walk the long way around to reach the small antique footbridge across the River Aire.

Continue along the towpath and you will soon arrive at the next turn bridge. This bridge once gave access to a small farm on the far bank named Rawcliffe. The bridge would have linked the farm to the track to Apperley Bridge before it was demolished. Passing by the site of another small demolished farm named Crow Croft you come to Thackley Canal Bridge. Here you enter the field to your left and head towards the first bridge underneath the railway. It is only a couple of hundred yards ahead.

Pass through here then head across the field towards an iron suspension bridge across the River Aire and the former Esholt Estate. This bridge is guarded at each end by twin iron pillars surmounted with crowns a larger version would not look out of place spanning a great river.

After crossing the bridge you head for The Avenue which lies somewhere dead ahead. Turn left here and pass by the office units of Home farm and before long you will have reached Gill Lane on the edge of the woods. Gill Lane was the old packhorse trail which the merchants would use to transport their goods from Esholt to Nether Yeadon and beyond.

You only climb the slight incline for a few hundred yards before turning off to your left to follow the line of the railway up towards Spring Woods.

Here, alongside Guiseley Beck you may see the scant remains of Waterloo Scribbling Mill. The beck runs through the trees along the bottom of a gully to the side of ancient Springs Road. A little further along Springs Road look down into the gully and can clearly see a natural basin alongside the beck. Even though it was now filled with trees you can make out the shape of the former millpond. Every mill needed a water source and a pond in which to store the water for further use when needed. Waterloo Mill will have been no different.

The wood at this point has thinned out and here there is plenty of light and this gives it a pastoral ambience rather than any dank and dark broodiness. Move through the wood in silence marvelling at the cobblestones still evident on the road.

How many horse-driven carts had travelled over these stones to and from the mill? Who were the people that drove them? Where and how did they live? Questions fill your mind as you continue along Springs Road towards the giant stone gateposts a little further on.

The stone gateposts stood at the entrance to a track that led off into the woods. Waterloo Mill would surely have been situated down here beside the dam of Guiseley Beck. This mill belonged to Esholt Estate and the old Ordnance Survey maps show it as a "Scribbling" mill. Scribbling was the process of preparing the raw fleece for spinning and includes the separation or "carding" of the wool fibres. This was traditionally done by children at home but upon the advent of mills, it was carried out in a more mechanised manner.

Here, the image of the heavy-laden carts piled high with dirty foul smelling fleeces lumbering down the road that you are stood on is hard not to imagine. After only a few hundred yards you cross under an old stone railway bridge and you are practically on top of the site of the famous Esholt rail crash.

The Esholt Junction rail crash occurred on Thursday 9 June 1892, at the point at which the Otley and Ilkley Joint Railway from Ilkley divides, one branch in the direction of Leeds and the other Bradford, a short distance after Guiseley railway station. Two trains collided at around three-thirty in the afternoon, resulting in the deaths of five passengers, and injuries to twenty-six more. The driver, fireman and guard of one of the trains were injured, as was a guard on the other train. Although vegetation obscuring a signal was accepted as the primary cause of the crash, a recommendation was made to alter certain signalling procedures at the junction to prevent a recurrence.

The crash arose as three trains neared the junction at much the same time — a common enough occurrence. From the direction of Bradford, a Bradford-Harrogate train was following a route taking it in the direction of Guiseley; from the Leeds branch, a Leeds-Ilkley train was also heading towards Guiseley; whilst in the other direction an Ilkley-Bradford train approached the junction from Guiseley.

Signalman Harry l'Anson, in the Esholt signal box, gave the Bradford-Harrogate train permission to pass the junction; meanwhile in the Apperley signal box, signalman Thomas Aubrey, knowing the Ilkley-Bradford train was approaching, gave the Leeds-Ilkley train permission to proceed towards the junction under a procedure called clause 16, which allowed trains to near the junction under the proviso that they were likely to encounter a danger signal before the junction proper.

At the junction, the Leeds-Ilkley driver, Archibald McLay, despite acknowledging that he had been given a clause 16 permission, and in spite of his four and a half year's service on the line, mistook the proceed signal given to the Bradford-Harrogate train as relating to his line. In fact, his signal was at danger, but obscured by vegetation at the time he looked at it. By the time his train arrived at the junction, it was being crossed by the Ilkley-Bradford train. The Ilkley-bound train ploughed through the last six carriages of the Bradford bound train, overturning the last of these; the engine and tender of the Ilkley bound train also turned over. Five passengers, all on the Ilkley-Bradford train died, one instantly, one en route to and three in hospital. Twenty-six passengers were injured and McLay and his fireman, Walter Bolton, received serious injuries, as did the guard on his train and one of the guards on the Bradford-bound train.

An investigation by Major General C. S. Hutchinson concluded that whereas the immediate cause was the obscured signal, signalling practice at Esholt Junction — specifically clause 16, which allowed trains to approach the junction simultaneously — should be abolished and considered to be a breach of the Regulation of Railways Act 1889. The Bradford junction signal was also repositioned so that it could not be seen from the Leeds line.

At this point you are firmly in Guiseley rather than Bradford, so with that in mind you have to make your way across the fields to Sodhall Hill and thence to Old Hollins Hill where you can make your way to Esholt village. Facing uphill on Springs Road you head to your left and walk until you reach Old Hollins Hill.

The road of Old Hollins Hill winds steeply downhill past the disused Hollins Hill Quarry towards a fine Victorian Viaduct on the edge of the village of Esholt.

Station Road leads you into the village which is correctly named as Upper Esholt. All will be still and quiet as you stand in the centre of this quintessentially English country village. With its tiny village shop, close cosy cottages, and pub it is little wonder that it is renowned the world over for its charm.

From the village centre you walk along Chapel Lane passing by Esholt Old Hall on your left. Originally belonging to the De Warde family the medieval Manor house is the oldest in the village. Now Grade II listed this stone-built jewel once even had a moat. The building dates back at least as far as the sixteenth century and some of its timber frame construction, with stud partitioning and altered king post roof trusses, has survived. This section may well incorporate part of the medieval hall that stood on the site.

The building is now an irregular structure, consisting of two storeys that were rebuilt by the Sherbourne family in the late sixteenth century and a taller two-storey and attic portion under one large gable that was built in the mid-seventeenth century by the Calverley family. The historical development of the building contributes greatly to its interest, demonstrating the changes in tastes and building techniques as the centuries proceeded.

The building is built of large blocks of coursed gritstone and has a stone slate roof with saddle stones to the gables. The attributes of the building are now mixed. The windows, for example, vary from the five-light and four-light chamfered mullioned windows with drip moulds on the mid-seventeenth century section, to the earlier square mullioned type. The tall chimney stacks that stand above the roofline contribute greatly to its stature and the clapper boarding of the gable wall is particularly unusual. Internally, too, the building has retained some rare and interesting features, such as the coffered oak ceiling of the parlour.

Many of the village's fine early 18th century workers cottages were used in the filming of the famous soap opera Emmerdale Farm or Emmerdale as it is known today. As you leave the village behind the cottages gave way to open fields containing horses grazing in the warm sun.

You pass by the late Georgian property named Home House and perhaps pause for a few moments at the bottom of Cunliffe Lane to admire the terrace houses of Bunkers Hill. These houses were known as Demdyke Row in Emmerdale.

Here at the end of Cunliffe Lane, there was once a Tannery served by forty stone pits and three springs to provide water for the tanning process.

You continue along the narrow and winding Esholt Lane past the site of the long-gone Upper Esholt Mill towards the final part of your walk. Following the path of the nearby river Aire alongside us, you come to the tiny settlement of Tarn with its 18th-century vernacular style workers cottages and Tarn Grange as its centre. This marvellous property contains a stone dated 1827. Opposite standing in splendid isolation amongst the fields is Bean House.

From here you can hear the cars rushing by on nearby Otley Road and this denotes the end of this particular walk. Here you can catch the 653 bus from Otley or the 737 Yorkshire Tiger bus back to Bradford Interchange to complete this walk.

Hodgson's Fold to Walnut Farm Via Peel Park

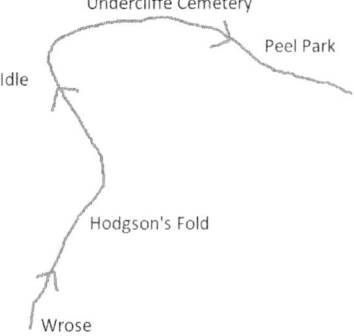

Everyone loves a time bubble if they can find one. A place where time stands still and all your cares and woes simply drift away leaving you in a state of suspended animation almost. A place where there are no modern inconveniences, no takeaways, shops or music blaring out. A place where modern life simply does not exist to a certain extent. It just happens that I know of a place that does and it is only five minutes walk from home.

To begin this walk you need to catch bus 612 or 633 from Bradford Interchange and get off at the stop opposite the five a side football pitches on Kings Road at Swaine House. The approximate distance for this walk is 3.0 miles.

When you depart from the bus turn around with the road at your back and look up the hill and through the modern houses in front of you. This whole area was once the site and the grounds of a sizeable Victorian mansion named Bolton Lodge.

Bolton Lodge was a gothic style mansion built by Wm. Stead in the 1850s on land adjoining Wood Lane Farm. The site had, before this, been a public garden kept by John Ackroyd, a local Wesleyan preacher, whose house had also stood on the site. There was an ornate cast iron lamp post by the kitchen door which stood in a rockery. The house stood on a terrace of level ground and had steps down to the gently sloping grounds surrounded by a perimeter wall with large trees. The outline of the Lodge grounds is still clearly defined by mature Sycamore trees.

From here you cross Kings Road and climb up the steep steps towards Old Hill. You join the footpath that runs along the top of Old Hill along the side of the present Hanson School playing fields. It is an ancient track that merchants once trod along their way across from Bolton on the other side of the hill. After perhaps a thousand yards the path forks down to the right into an estate and left towards the time bubble of Hodgson Fold. It is quite an innocuous start as the path skirts alongside the huge side of the 18th-century house on one side and a grass bank on the other and after thirty yards or so you come to a stone stile at the end of the footpath.

This is known as a Kissing Gate and the word has evolved from the ancient word "Kisting". These stones are arranged in such a way as to form a solid wall, and when looked at from near ground level by cattle and sheep it would appear to form a solid obstacle. Possessing only two-dimensional sight this tricks the animals into believing there is no way through, whilst humans with their three-dimensional sight can see the opening.

After squeezing through the narrow gap you enter the marvellous and evocative place that is Hodgson's Fold. The diminutive former agricultural hamlet of Hodgson Fold is located in the neighbourhood of Bolton, which is located approximately two miles to the northeast of Bradford city centre. Hodgson Fold was one of a number of tiny hamlets located in this ancient township and mentioned in the Domesday Survey it is thought to have Anglo-Saxon origins.

Little is known of the form or size of Hodgson Fold until the first reliable maps of the 18th century were created. However, documentary evidence suggests that a settlement developed at Hodgson Fold around the mid-17th century when several buildings, including a house dated 1652, were constructed.

It seems likely that John Hodgson, whose initials are inscribed over the door of the dated house, gave his name to the hamlet. The Hodgson family continued to live in the Fold for the next three hundred years. The township of Bolton was renowned locally for its beef and dairy products, which supplied the surrounding towns and villages. Records show that as well as farmers and farmhands, a number of Worsted and cloth weavers lived in Hodgson Fold in the late 18th century. Historical records indicate that they worked from the upper rooms of the cottages that were demolished in the late 19th century.

By the late 18th century, records show a diversification in the occupations of the residents of Hodgson Fold, with a move away from agriculture. Several members of the Hodgson family became butchers by profession. It is reputed that the upper rooms of several cottages were used for weaving by Messrs Ackroyd and Lightfoot. This venture into small-scale textile manufacture was common in many agricultural areas during the late 18th century. However, once the production of textiles moved into the mills, hand weaving, and spinning became swiftly uneconomical.

It is likely that the main source of employment returned to agriculture during the 19th century as the demand for fresh dairy and beef production increased in the growing town of Bradford.

Until the middle of the 19th century, the land at Hodgson Fold remained in the ownership of the Hodgson family. The Ordnance Survey map of 1852 shows the Fold at the end of a long narrow lane and surrounded by fields. The form and size of the hamlet is not much different to that of today, though the later Victorian developments had yet to be built. In 1854, following the death of the principal landowner, John Hodgson, his substantial estate was split between his three offspring – John Hodgson Jnr, Mrs J. Atkinson-Jowett, and Mrs Crowther.

Upon his wife's inheritance James Atkinson- Jowett took up residence in the hamlet. A large Italianate residence called Grove House was built to the northeast of Hodgson Fold and the old cottages along the lane demolished to make way for a pair of villa houses c. 1870. A formal carriageway was laid linking Grove House to Myers Lane.

By 1891, James Hodgson Jowett-Atkinson was the largest landowner in Bolton and one of most affluent men in Bradford. After the Second World War, there was much residential development around the township of Bolton. Many of the tiny rural hamlets that made up the township were surrounded or enveloped by these new housing estates. Hodgson Fold was not an exception to this and now stands amidst the Ashbourne and Grove House estates.

Stand there in the centre of this tiny hamlet and take in a series of deep breaths. Your nostrils twitch upon sensing freshly baked bread. Perhaps somewhere in one of the small cottages a little old lady in an apron is baking bread on her old coal blacked wood-fired oven perhaps. Look around for the source.

Although it is only small the cottages seem to step back to create a feeling of endless openness. Intoxicated by the unworldly aroma of the baking bread you walk through the tiny passageway between two cottages at the bottom of the courtyard. Here the humble dwellings are close enough for the residents to shake hands across the cobbled pathway.

Stop to admire the initials JH carved in the stone above the doorway of his first house in Hodgson's Fold. To your right ivy grows and fingers its way around the mullioned windows of yet another timeless cottage. Here before you is an open door and the heavenly smell of yeast and bread wafts out along the street as if to entice passing weary travellers to come and rest ye a while and feast.

Hodgson's Fold is so small you can walk around it in about thirty seconds so you have to do it twice and then once more again. Round and round you go, your head spinning with images of old farmers in flat caps and heavy boots, the smell of newly cut grass forcing my imagination into overdrive. In your head you are back in the 18th century, you are feeling it, living it and loving it.

There is a well-tended patch of garden to the rear of the centre of the tiny courtyard. To which cottage it belongs I know not and perhaps it is a communal space. It sits behind a stout drystone wall and is entered by a small metal gate. This was the local pinfold. The marvellous cottage "Fieldhead" stands opposite and is flanked on one side by the rear of a converted Grade II listed barn and by the gabled front of the 17th-century cottage of number fourteen on the other.

When you have had your fill of the fold it is time to depart for Myers Lane and onwards to Bolton Outlanes.

Myers Lane was named after the local Myers family but before that, it was called Owl Lane. The Myers built houses on the lane and were occupied by Cartwrights and Cow Doctors. One family member Joseph Myers (known as Dozy Doll) was employed as the local "Pinder". A Pinder was a man who would round up the local straying cattle and sheep and place them in the local pinfold to await collection by their owners.

Glance over to your left at the green playing fields that slope up the hillside towards Hanson school. This building sits on top of the hill overlooking Hodgson Fold. The school, which was built during the 1970s, was constructed on the site of Grove House, the Victorian villa built for James Atkinson-Jowett in 1860. The lodge for the house still stands at the end of Grove House Road and gives some idea of what Grove House would have looked like before it was demolished in the 1950s. You pass by the lodge as we walked steadily up the slight incline towards the Swing Gate public house.

Standing in the car park of the pub you can marvel at Bolton's oldest building, the superb Ivy Hall. Constructed in 1616 and owned at one time by John Bailey it has a large buttressed chimney with steps on the inside for sweeps to use whilst cleaning it. Bailey also owned the Tollbooth and prison which once stood at the junction of Ivegate and Kirkgate in Bradford. A local legend states that a tunnel once led from here to Bolling Hall. Why Ivy Hall stands side by side with the rear of William Morrison's first Supermarket is anyone's guess!

Passing through Bolton Junction next to the now sadly disappeared pub The Junction, you walk along Idle Road for a while. This long straight road will take you all the way to your next port of call. After passing by The Malt Kiln you reach the junction with otley Road and turn right to approach one of England's greatest Victorian Cemeteries.

Rivalled only by Highgate Cemetery in London, Undercliffe Cemetery is an absolute marvel of Victorian Funerailia and a visit there is always a joy.

The cemetery stands atop a hillside overlooking the city and contains some very impressive Victorian monuments in a variety of styles. It is a notable example of a Victorian cemetery where a number of rich and prominent local residents have been buried, notably mill owners and former mayors.

Undercliffe Cemetery is Grade II listed by English Heritage in their Register of Parks and Gardens of Special Historic Interest in England. In the early 1800s Bradford's textile industry underwent rapid growth and with it Bradford's population, consequently, there was pressure on housing then on burial ground space and this eventually became a health hazard.

As a result, many of the existing cemeteries were closed by order of Bradford Council. Partly in response to this situation the 'Bradford Cemetery Company' was set up and provisionally registered in 1849. Membership of the company included local notables Henry Brown, Robert Milligan, William Rand, Edward Ripley and Sir Titus Salt. The land used for the cemetery had previously been agricultural land with a farmhouse on the part of the Undercliffe Estate owned by the Hustler family. The plot was purchased in 1851 by John Horsfall for £3,400 and he founded The Bradford Cemetery Company in 1852.

The cemetery was designed and laid out over the years 1851–1854 by park and cemetery designer William Gay (1814–1893) and architect John Dale for the sum of £12,000 for landscaping, planting, and building involving the construction in 1854 of two chapels on the main promenade.

The cemetery is at a height of 210 m above sea level with an area of 26 acres accommodating some 124,000 burials and about 23,000 marked graves. A major feature of the cemetery is the long east-west promenade with the western end having excellent views over Bradford. Also at the western end is a small bandstand. Most of the western half of the site is consecrated for Anglican burials while the eastern half is set aside for non-conformist burials such as Baptist, Methodist, and Quaker.

The Quaker graves are characterised by their identical horizontal ground level memorial stones. The northern area of the cemetery was set aside for the unbaptised and those who had been excommunicated or committed suicide. Communal graves known as 'company plots' are to be found on the southern side of the site where up to thirty coffins at a time were interred in one grave.

The monuments are extremely thought-provoking even if one or two are now in need of repair and three graves in particular are worth paying a visit.

Alfred Angas Scott (1875-1923) was a British motorcycle designer, inventor and founder of the Scott Motorcycle Company. A prolific inventor, he took out over 50 patents between 1897 and 1920, mostly concerning two-stroke engines and road vehicles. Scott was a keen potholer and the second president of the Gritstone Club. In July 1923, Scott travelled back to Bradford in his open Scott Sociable wearing wet potholing clothes and contracted pneumonia from which he died.

Alfred Scott's first motorcycle was developed from his own two horsepower twin-cylinder engine design which he hand-built and fitted to the steering head of a bicycle. These engines were used to power equipment such as lathes and light machinery and Scott had been involved in the manufacture of 'Premier' pedal cycles. He developed this prototype into a motorcycle and six were produced under contract by friends with a car company called Jowett in Bradford.

Scott patented an early form of calliper brakes in 1897, and designed a fully triangulated frame, rotary induction valves, and used unit construction for his motorcycle engine. Scott started making boat engines in 1900. He patented his first engine in 1904 and started motorcycle production in 1908 with a vertical two-stroke 450 cc twin, with patented triangulated frame, chain drive, neutral-finder, kick starter and a two-speed gearbox. His patented two-stroke engine designs are still the basis of modern two-stroke engines and features such as the first kick start, mono-shock suspension, efficient radiators, rotary inlet valves, drip-feed lubricators, and centre stands also remain today.

The second grave is that of Stafford Heginbotham, the local businessman and the Chairman of Bradford City Football Club at the time of the fire in 1985. In 1971, Heginbotham set-up the Bradford-based company Tebro Toys. Six years later the Bradford Telegraph & Argus had quoted Heginbotham as saying "I have just been unlucky" after the business suffered two major fires in succession. Heginbotham became chairman of Bradford City football club, where he was a popular figure, the current official mascot for Bradford City A.F.C. was introduced by Heginbotham in 1966, the 'City Gent' character being modelled on him. He was credited with saying that 'Football is the Opera of the people".

In 1995, following a heart transplant operation at St George's Hospital in Tooting, Heginbotham died. His funeral was held at Bradford Cathedral in early May 1995 and he was interred at the west end of the east-west promenade at overlooking Valley Parade.

The last of the three graves stands in a quite neglected area where trees grow wild and thick and bushes are all around. It stands somewhere in the bushes about midway between Heginbothams grave and Otley Road. If you can manage to locate it then you can kneel before the final resting place of a true English hero. A man like they don't make any more who braved the Russian cannons at Sebastopol and lived to tell the tale. In fact, he lived to own and run a humble beer and lodging house at 147 Wapping Road not far from the cemetery but that does not detract from his obvious bravery in The Crimean War.

Matthew Hughes VC (1822 – 9 January 1882) was an English recipient of the Victoria Cross, the highest and most prestigious award for gallantry in the face of the enemy that can be awarded to British and Commonwealth forces. Hughes was approximately 33 years old and a private in 7th Regiment of Foot (now The Royal Regiment of Fusiliers), British Army when, during the Crimean War, he performed the acts that saw him recommended for the VC. The full citation was in the first set of awards of the VC published in the London Gazette on 24 February 1857, and read:

"War Office, 24th February 1857. The Queen has been graciously pleased to signify Her intention to confer the decoration of the Victoria Cross on the undermentioned Officers and Men of Her Majesty's Navy and Marines, and Officers, Non-commissioned Officers, and Men of Her Majesty's Army, who have been recommended to Her Majesty for that Decoration, in accordance with the rules laid down in Her Majesty's Warrant of the 29th of January, 1856 on account of acts of bravery performed by them before the Enemy during the late War, as recorded against their several names, viz. :—7th Regiment No. 1879 Private Mathew Hughes

Private Mathew Hughes, the 7th Royal Fusiliers, was noticed by Colonel Campbell, 90th Light Infantry, on the 7th June 1855, at the storming of the Quarries, for twice going for ammunition, under a heavy fire, across the open ground; he also went to the front, and brought in Private John Hampton, who was lying severely wounded; and on the 18th June 1855, he volunteered to bring in Lieutenant Hobson, 7th Royal Fusiliers, who was lying severely wounded, and, in the act of doing so, was severely wounded himself".

Queen Victoria presented Hughes with his VC IN Hyde Park on the 26th of June 1857. The English hero Matthew Hughes VC died at Wapping in Bradford aged 60 on 9th June 1882

If you can locate his grave sit a while in the grass at the side of one so brave. You are alongside the mortal remains of a man who was far braver than most men could ever hope to be. He had, with his own eyes witnessed and partaken in events that we today cannot even begin to comprehend. Rest in peace brave old soldier your stint is done.

After bidding Matthew Hughes farewell, you now walk the short distance to the Otley road exit and leave the cemetery. You are now heading for the famous Peel Park but not before noticing a strange set of two stone steps at the side of the pavement further down on the left. A rather bizarre place to have the mounting steps for an 18th-century carriage. From here you cross over the road and enter Bradford's first public park.

Peel Park is a 56-acre urban public park in the Bolton and Undercliffe area of Bradford, England, located about 0.75 miles north-east of the city centre. A public meeting took place in St George's Hall, Bradford on 13 August 1850 to discuss the creation of a park as a memorial to Sir Robert Peel who had died that year. Together with a government donation of £1,500, funding was raised from Sir Robert Milligan, Sir Titus Salt, Forbes, and Company and by numerous other private subscriptions to purchase 64 acres of land that was subsequently named Peel Park Estate, and some 56 acres of this land was developed as Peel Park. The park was opened in 1853 and a series of galas were held in the park to raise funds to pay off the remaining debt for the purchase of the land and its layout as a park—this took some 12 years. In 1870, the park was conveyed to the Municipal Borough of Bradford and is now owned by the City of Bradford.

In 1902, an ornamental bandstand was erected midway along The Terrace and today this location is occupied by the statue of Sir Robert Peel. Another lost feature is the two cannons captured by the British in the Crimean War. The park had a total of four drinking fountains but two have subsequently been lost. The park had its own plant nursery south of the northwestern entrance at Bolton Road with computer-controlled greenhouses but this property was sold off for commercial use reducing the park's area. In 1997 100 trees were planted in the park and this is commemorated by a stone plaque on a boulder near the southern entrance.

The southern Cliffe Road entrance has ornate gates and a lodge (1861) but larger and more impressive are the main gates and lodge (1862) at the northern Bolton Road entrance. There are two grade II listed two-storey Italianate lodges, one at the park gates on Bolton Road and a smaller lodge to a similar design at the Cliffe Road entrance. The main linear path through the park is The Terrace extending east-west on which can be found a number of statues. One such is a statue of Sir Robert Peel made in 1855 and dressed in a mid-19th-century frock coat and mounted on a cylindrical ashlar sandstone plinth.

At the western end of The Terrace is the Viewing Platform (1853–93) giving views over the Bradford valley and Manningham. The platform was largely rebuilt in 1990 due to its poor condition. A cast-iron bridge (1857) takes the eastern end of The Terrace over the carriage drive. The cast-iron bridge beams are embossed with the words "RAILWAY-FOUNDRY. BRADFORD. 1857. Close to the Bolton Road entrance, adjacent to formal gardens is a 'distorted figure-of-eight' shaped lake with two islands and a variety of waterfowl. The island in the east of the lake is so large relatively that the lake takes on a serpentine appearance.

When you reach the Bolton Road exit of the park you cross over Bolton Road and walk down Bolton Lane, passing by the ancient hamlet of Low Fold towards the even more ancient Walnut Farm. This beautiful farmhouse and cottage has stood in its present location for centuries and has at times been known as Bartlett House, Bolton Banks Farm, Bolton Fold and Walnut Tree Farm. In 1651, it was in the possession of John Jowett of Ye Olde Kirkgate Bradford. On the gable of the house are the initials B.E.B and the date 1736.

These represent the names of Benjamin Bartlett and his wife Elizabeth who built the new house as a summer residence. A Walnut tree was planted here in the 1700s and by 1812 the tree was fully matured and according to records produced 100's of Walnuts each season.

Built in 1736 by Benjamin Bartlett the Bradford apothecary, this two-storey farmhouse and the lower adjoining cottage is built from irregular coursed sandstone with Gritstone and flush quoins and stone slate roofs. The gable ends of the farmhouse have parapet copings rising from shaped kneelers, four-light chamfered mullions and a central mullioned transomed stair light. The famous executioner James Berry died here at Walnut farm on 21st October 1913 aged 61. He was the executioner who failed to hang John Babbacombe Lee – "The Man They Couldn't Hang" – in 1885. The trap door repeatedly failed to open and Lee's sentence was commuted.

From Walnut Farm, it is but a short walk down to Kings Road where you can catch either the 612 or 633 bus back to Bradford Interchange to complete this walk.

This walk begins at St. Lukes Church on Harrogate Road at the junction with Pullan Avenue in Eccleshill. To reach this spot you can catch buses 645, 660, 670 or 747 from Bradford Interchange. The approximate distance for this walk is 4.1 miles.

St. Lukes Church itself was built and consecrated in 1848 and was designed in a largely Gothic style with a spire. This spire however, was removed circa 1971 and was later rebuilt in a more modern style when the stonework began crumbling. That explains the clash of styles. Just behind the church on Fagley Lane is Fagley School which was built in 1842.

From the church you cross the road towards a solid looking row of 18th century Weavers cottages called Armscliffe Place and make your way along Victoria Road towards the village of Eccleshill. Victoria Road was formerly known as Mill Lane and was given its present-day name in 1887 in honour of Queen Victoria's Golden Jubilee. Parts of this area was quarried in the 18th century for the stone which was used in the construction of many of the local fine mills and buildings.

In Roman times the Eccleshill area was crossed by two lanes. One lane was along what is now Norman Lane and the other to Apperley Bridge down the road now known as Bank. After the Norman Conquest the lands of Eccleshill were given to William, Earl of Warren. In 1274 ownership of lands passed to the Sheffields and in 1407 to the Bolling family of Calverley then the Scargills, Saviles, Wyatts, Zouches, Stanhopes, Hirds, and then to Jeremiah Rawson.

In the Middle Ages Eccleshill was shunned by church authorities after a supposed incident in which it is said a preacher or monk was stoned to death on the main road through Eccleshill village. This supposed incident is said to be the reason behind naming the main road 'Stony Lane'. The real explanation may be that either the road was stony or that it led on to Stone Hall.

You soon pass Old Mill on the left, an early 1800's woollen mill which was rebuilt in 1816 after being destroyed by fire. The present building on the site is dated 1863 although parts of it date back to the early 1800s.

A short distance on you arrive at a triangular junction in the road. Here on the right stood Hutton school. This fine Victorian building was built in 1886 by local mill owner John Hutton on land where Old Eccleshill Hall once stood. Today only the gateposts of the Hall situated in the wall surrounding the Hutton School site remain.

John Hutton bought the land in 1884 for £2000 and donated it so the school bearing his name could be built there. The world famous artist and former Eccleshill resident David Hockney studied here in his youth.

Directly opposite Hutton School is the well-known local landmark known as the "Monkey Bridge". Sitting underneath a stone-paved walkway in a large stone wall the Monkey Bridge was a 19th-century village lock-up for drunks and also a public urinal. Just in front of here was a grassy triangular junction upon which stood the village stocks. Presumably, the drunks served time in the stocks as well as the lock-up. The stocks were moved in later years to nearby Hodgson's Fold.

From this point you continue on Victoria Road towards the old Methodist Chapel which sits just at the rear of The Victoria Inn at Bank Top. The steep road leading down to Harrogate Road from Bank Top, known as Bank, is an ancient road that dates back to Roman times.

In 1775, this small Chapel also known as Bank Top Chapel was constructed on Lands Lane off Norman Lane. The famous Methodist John Wesley (1703-1791) preached here in 1776 it is said. The building was in use as a chapel until 1854 and today it is one of the oldest buildings in Eccleshill. It was the third Methodist Chapel to be built in the city of Bradford. On the opposite side of Norman Lane is the Chapel burial ground which was created in 1823. This hallowed ground contains one interesting grave

This particular grave contains the mortal remains of one Donald Jowett. Sgt Pilot Jowett died aged 20 aboard a Consolidated PBY Catalina MK II AM269 BN-K flying boat aircraft, which crashed shortly after take-off near to Stranraer in Scotland. Jowett was a member of 240 Squadron RAF which was based nearby at Loch Ryan.

Further along Norman Lane directly opposite The Lane Ends public house is a building which is obviously a converted cinema, or Picture House to use its correct term for the period. Despite today being used as a gym and health centre it has that particular aesthetic appearance that old cinemas always seem to have.

The Palladium Cinema was opened in 1929 by Ralph Dickinson and upon construction had 1,000 seats in stalls and circle levels. In 1931 the new owner John Lambert of Modern theatres changed the name to The Regal and reduced the seating capacity to 900. The Regal Cinema was closed on 23rd November 1966 with the final offering being the great Peter Cushing and the majestic Christopher Lee in "The Hound of the Baskervilles", and Leo Genn in the film "Steel Bayonet".

The building was then changed into a bingo hall, which operated until 1988 when it was converted into a Snooker club. In 2008, the snooker club closed and this area was taken over by the gymnasium in 2009. Today it houses an independently run fitness centre named Flacks Fitness.

This walk includes a visit to Bolton Old Hall at the end of Wood Lane, so from the former picture house you head along Wrose Road until you reach the junction with Kings road. Turn left here and continue on for four hundred yards before turning right onto Wood Lane.

What remains of Wood lane was once part of the ancient packhorse track from Idle via Idle Moor down to Bradford. The farmers and merchants would use this trail to transport their goods and livestock to the market in Bradford. After a short distance, it ends as a road and becomes more of a footpath which still winds its way down the side of Bolton Woods quarry to the site of the long-dismantled set of locks for the Bradford Canal which was known as "Oliver's Lock". At the point where it changes to a footpath, stop for a second or two to admire a quaint 18th-century farmstead building to your left.

This solid structure of typical vernacular Sandstone construction was built in 1857 by the local Jowett family. No doubt some distant relations of Sgt Pilot Donald. The building was converted into four separate cottages sometime in the early 19th century and was then home to workers from the estate of the nearby Bolton Lodge.

From this point you head directly across the adjacent two fields where you will find Bolton Old Hall in the far right-hand corner. This Grade II listed coursed Gritstone timber-framed hall house was built in 1627 for a wealthy wool merchant. The north front has a large mullioned-transomed window lighting the staircase. The Doorway has a date panel inscribed "TW over Anno Doi" above the date 1627.

According to local legend, the house is haunted by "Blue Mary". This apparition appears at the circular window in the upper wall of the main gabled front section of the house. Past residents of the house have said that she was causing the decline in the local cow's ability to produce milk and what little milk was produced was rancid, so they hung up horseshoes and needles to placate her.

A short distance away we joined Bolton Hall Road on its way down to the village of Bolton Woods. This is the small track between Bolton Old Hall and the football pitches that border Wrose Road. After a few yards take a small detour to your right down into a small gully, where at the bottom one of Bradford's "Holy Wells" breaks the surface. Today this tiny trickle of water known as Trap Sike runs down the valley side to ultimately join Bradford Beck on Canal Road.

Rejoining Bolton Hall Road we walked down the steeply narrow heavily tree-lined road, past the entrance to Bolton Woods Quarry and a small row of former quarry workers cottages to emerge in bright sunlight by The New Vic public house. In the early days of Bolton Woods village, this was The Conservative Club and was subsequently owned and run by Walkers Bradford Breweries. On the gable end of the pub there remains a faded "ghost sign" promoting this famed local brewery.

You are now on Stanley Road and heading out of the village in the general direction of Canal Road. On the first slight bend in the road almost on the edge of what was once a small but quite dense plantation named Bolton Woods there stands one of the ventilation stacks for the Frizinghall to Esholt sewage tunnel.

This is one of three such stacks along the length of this three-mile long tunnel linking the long gone Frizinghall sewage treatment works with the newly built facility at Esholt. The second stack is a short way back past Bolton Woods village and the third is behind the clubhouse of the cricket ground on Westfield Lane at Idle. This tunnel was started in 1913 but was interrupted by WWI before being finished in the 1920s. The Frizinghall plant which treated the raw sewage was closed in 1926 and only a few huge pipes running along Bradford Beck remain today.

From here you walk up Poplars Park Road towards the site of the part built new housing estate climb over a stout stone wall to the right to enter the small wooded copse that once contained the farm and house named Hollin Close. Over the years since the demise of these buildings, nature has reclaimed the area and today the trees are tightly packed forming a dense canopy that blots out the sunlight. This gives it a gloomy and somewhat edgy atmosphere despite it being so close to modern-day housing. The thickness of the trees and vegetation seem to form an impenetrable wall that keeps out any nearby sounds.

The house and farm of Hollin Close was once owned by the Jowett family and then in turn by the Rawson family, before being leased in the latter part of last century to the corn dealer William Oliver. During his time at Hollin Close, some of the land was required for the soon to be built Bradford Canal. The land was to be used for the construction of one of the canal locks. This lock, which was one of ten such locks on the canal came to be known as Oliver's Locks.

Bradford Canal closed to navigation in 1922 and the site here is now home to various industrial units. A small stream which runs down the valley side from Old Hill behind The Horse and Farrier pub to Bradford Beck is known as Oliver's Beck. In 1852, Hollin Close was leased to a tea dealer named John Tordoff who manufactured starch in the outbuildings. Today apart from a few small walls almost nothing remains of the house and farm that once was Hollin Close.

After stumbling through the undergrowth of the Hollin Close site for a while you must find the scant and faint outline traces of the carriage drive for the house and follow this away from the site. Somewhere in this area, there is reputed to be a number of very old gravestones lying flat in the soil. These cover a burial pit containing some victims of a medieval Smallpox epidemic.

After crossing over the culvert that crosses Oliver's Beck and skirting around what remains of Brow Wood you emerge at the bottom end of Bolton Lane. Turning uphill you walk the short distance to Kings Road then bare right to make for the small nature reserve which runs alongside towards the site of the former Spink Well Locks.

This nature reserve was created in the early 1990s from derelict land and is a haven for a variety of wildlife species such as Long Tailed Tits, Greenfinch, and even Orange Tip Butterflies. Kestrels nest on the site each year and can often be seen hunting over the hillside. Here you will find most of the original huge carved stone blocks which formed part of the Spink Well canal lock. The stones were dumped in the dense thick undergrowth in this area when the lock was dismantled in 1922.

Today the Citroen car dealership on the very end of Kings Road covers the site of the lock. It will not take you long to discover the two massive piles of moss-covered blocks of carved stone. They simply lay at the side of the path under a canopy of overhanging wild trees. Due to their immense size and weight they will not have moved since they were placed there nearly a century before.

The whole area around here has changed immensely in that time. The huge Power Station on Canal Road and the massive gas holders next to the canal bridge have long gone. Numerous modern and brightly lit car showrooms have replaced these dour and grimy industrial buildings.

But sitting atop the dismantled canal lock stones in this inner-city haven of peace you can almost hear the greetings of long-deceased canal boatmen as they approached the lock.

In 1939, many years after the canal had fallen into disuse, a local lad aged ten named Leonard Partridge drowned when he fell into the disused Spink Well Lock. By then the lock served no purpose and sometimes tempted local children to play in and around it. Leonard laid on a plank and tried to reach a piece of timber that was floating in the middle of the water and sadly he slipped in.

Here you can end this walk and catch either bus 612 or bus 633 back to Bradford Interchange.

Fagley to Apperley Bridge

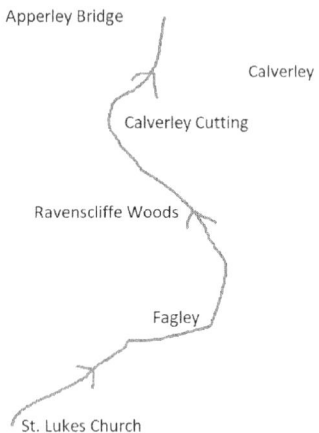

Apperley Bridge

Calverley

Calverley Cutting

Ravenscliffe Woods

Fagley

St. Lukes Church

There is a multitude of wooded areas in the Bradford area in which to walk. Some are dark and dense and some are light and open but they all have one thing in common. With a little imagination you can feel the past and the history of these places, and with a little knowledge, you can almost see how the people from centuries past lived and worked in these noblest of surroundings.

Woods and forests are alive even though there appears to be not much going on. They are the habitats of many living creatures and of course even the trees are alive. They grow slowly and relentlessly but they are alive all the same.

Even the present-day fields that surround the area were thick with forests four hundred years ago. Wild Deer and Boars roamed through the thick trees. They hunted and were themselves hunted until man laid the forests bare to make the fields you see around you today. A forest tells a story not only of evolution but of innovation. A story of man's quest to progress and better himself.

A beck that runs through a wood powered a waterwheel. The waterwheel powered a saw that cut the trees that had been felled by a man's labour. Where there was a forest there was always water and where there was water there was always power.

Man learned to harness it all to his advantage. A forest tells a story and on this walk you visit Ravenscliffe Woods, an ancient forest which tells many stories.

Once again this walk begins outside the church of St. Luke on Harrogate Road in Eccleshill. To reach here you can catch the 645, 660, 670 or 747 bus from Bradford interchange. The approximate distance for this walk is 4.2 miles.

From St. James church you head down Harrogate Road and almost immediately you arrive at Union Mills. Built by James Johnson in 1816 this steam powered two-storey mill was constructed for the Woollen trade. Sometime later Jeremiah Scott added a further three-storey extension. From 1892- 1983 John Pilley and Sons operated the mill and so it became known as "Pilley's Mill". In 1905, a serious fire destroyed much of the building but it was rebuilt and manufacture continued. Today the buildings are a mixture of commercial and light industrial units.

Continue on from the mill and very soon you meet Wharnecliffe drive on your right. Walk down here and turn left on Wharnecliffe Grove and continue to walk directly to the bottom where you can access the old railway trackbed. This will lead you down to Fagley.

The railway passed over nearby Harrogate Road by a bridge on its way over to Quarry Gap junction in Laisterdyke. The bridge was demolished many years ago when the road was widened. In 1874, the Great Northern Railway opened its Laisterdyke to Shipley branch railway, a six-mile double track branch line from Quarry Gap to Shipley and Windhill railway Station. The line passed through Eccleshill, Idle and Thackley stations on its way from Quarry Gap.

Eccleshill station opened in 1875 and was located just north of the bridge over Harrogate Road, but like the other stations, it was demolished many years ago when the line was closed. Today only the embankment and the abutment of one side of the bridge remains. The line was closed to passengers in 1931 although goods traffic continued until 1964. Sections of the former trackbed survive today though and it is a short part of this route that you now stand on.

As you walk along the narrow corridor of dried packed mud it is not difficult to imagine the steam Locomotive chugging along here on its way to Quarry Gap junction. Pulling three or maybe four packed carriages of dark-suited people, it laboured along the line. The steam rising upwards as the metallic noise of wheels on rails reverberating between the embankments alongside.

Excited children on perhaps their first train journey, laughed and cheered with joy at the novelty of it all. But today, a century and a half later all is quiet. The only children you will hear are those playing in the nearby council house gardens that back onto the former trackbed.

After a short distance, you will notice in the bushes part of a small stone wall to your right. Upon closer inspection you will find that it is the top of a bridge. There is a trail leading down from the side of the embankment onto a track below. The bridge runs underneath the former railway line giving access to fields on both sides. This was built upon the construction of the line to enable the local farmer to lead his cattle or sheep from one field to the next and therefore avoiding the railway line. How very pleasant and thoughtful of The Great Northern Railway Company.

You leave the line a little further on and let the path meander on towards Thornbury. Here you join the bottom part of Fagley Road and head down to where you can begin your trek through Ravenscliffe Woods. You pass by Ravenscliffe Farm cottage with its old barn and mullioned windows before arriving at a building that was obviously a former lodge.

In the garden of this small lodge is the most admirable cast-iron lamppost. Standing the height of two men with four individual ornate lamps at the crown it wouldn't have looked out of place in Kensington but here on the edge of one of Bradford's most notorious council estates, it looked distinctly out of place. I also noticed the most wonderful antique Victorian Postbox stood silently and somewhat forlorn in the garden. The things you can see in the most unexpected places when you wander around Bradford.

This lodge was one of four built as entrances to a new estate of luxury villas that were to be constructed in Calverley Wood. Designed in the 1850s the others were Apperley Lodge, or "The Needles Eye" as it was known, Carr Lodge and South Lodge. The Needles Eye was demolished in the 1960s on safety grounds.

With the 19th-century expansion of the region's manufacturing industries, nearby Calverley's situation within reach of the centre of Bradford made it a popular place for wealthy Bradford industrialists to live.

Fred Foster, Lord Mayor of Bradford, lived for a time in Ferncliffe House while the great industrialist and innovator Samuel Cunliffe-Lister was born at Calverley House Farm. The houses of Elmwood and Brookleigh were also occupied by prominent families.

In an effort to capitalise on this trend, in the 1850s, the Thornhill Estate devised a plan to lay out portions of land in Calverley Wood to be developed as a select housing development for wealthy industrialists. Expressions of interest were received and the roads were laid out, but just two plots were sold and developed before the scheme was abandoned. However, the scheme had a considerable impact on the appearance of the village, as stone quarried from Calverley Cutting was used in the construction of some of the village's houses.

Passing through the open ornate wrought iron gates beside the lodge you now enter the wood. The track before you was once the carriage drive which linked this part of the abandoned estate to the other on the far side of New Line at Greengates.

It was more than just a simple track though as you can see the remains of low sturdy walls which once lined the sides as it wound its way down through the woods. Back in the 1850s this area was nothing like it is today with the nearby Council estate running alongside. It will have been a rich and sumptuous wooded area where the wealthy industrialists of Bradford came to relax and enjoy the peacefulness within its boundaries. There lies the reason for the proposed development of the luxury villas.

As you pass through the woods the trees rise up alongside a huge soil banking to the right. This was held in place by a stout wall running for hundreds of yards. Here the wood supports a number of species of trees- Sessile Oak, Silver Birch, Sycamore, Beech, Rowen, and Ash to name but a few.

Down a gully to the left, Fagley Beck appears to follow you, silently watching our every move. Here, you may notice a small series of stepping stones over the beck. Smooth and well worn by tens of thousands of feet over the centuries, the flat stones lay across the beck as they had always done. The clear water trickles away on its journey to join the river Aire as you wave it goodbye.

Continue along the side of the beck and you will notice that the trees thin out in front of you to reveal an open meadow. Flat in nature but still surrounded with trees this was the site of a long-gone reservoir. Belonging to Bradford Corporation Waterworks it formed part of a nearby sewage farm. Today the stone-lined side walls and spillway are still visible through the vegetation. It was known as Low Rein Reservoir and was filled in after a series of drownings some years ago. Today nature has reclaimed the area and it has reverted back to woodland and the meadow you see before you.

From this point you follow Fagley Beck away from the meadow and towards Round Wood directly opposite the reservoir. This area was the site of a Medieval Ironworks. At this point, the beck was dammed to provide a head of water which was then used to power drop hammers to forge the iron into basic implements of all descriptions. The woods, the water, the power remember? Charcoal for heating the metal to the high temperatures needed was made from wood collected from the surrounding forest.

Now you rejoin the former carriage drive and continue walking until you enter Bill Wood. This will lead you to Ravenscliffe Mill.

Built by James Harper in 1872, this mill specialised in the manufacture of cloth for Army uniforms. Initially, this included scarlet tunics such as those worn by the British Army during the Anglo-Zulu conflict, but as the nation entered the Boer Wars production changed to Khaki and continued up to 1957 when production ceased due to lack of demand for such cloth. The mill is still operational today and has a number of uses including a gym.

You are now approaching another "time bubble", the tiny hamlet of Carr Bottom. To find this you have to rejoin the beck which runs on the far side of the large mill. Tucked away at the end of a small lane just off New Line and Carr Road, this collection of two cottages around a ford over Fagley Beck is but a world away from the modern hustle and bustle nearby.

The two small stone houses either side of the ford are listed buildings dating from the period 1650-1700, a time when building outside Calverley village and along the Carr was just starting. Both houses have unusually large lateral chimney stacks. Fagley Beck runs under the track between them and over this is a structure which is no more than a footbridge. In fact, it is marked on the 1847 Ordnance Survey map as such.

Down this track would come all the traffic, pedestrians, carriages and carts which passed up and down the valley between Leeds and the towns and villages in the Aire Valley. It was an awkward stretch of road and was probably unsuitable for stagecoaches until the New Line at Greengates was constructed 1826.

There are no satellite dishes, no parked cars nor any sign of modern life whatsoever within this tiny hamlet. The water from the beck rushed at some speed below your feet and makes a tremendous roar. This only adds to the ambience of this quaint tucked away piece of the past.

Rest a while here and try to picture an old man in his Grandad collar shirt tending the small garden of his cottage. It is the year 1860 and nearby Ravenscliffe Mill is yet to be built. The surrounding area is thick with mature trees and the air silent but for the sound of his digging. He is sowing potatoes that would feed him through the autumn. Simple peasant food but tasting all the better for being planted then harvested by his own hands.

He would feel good as he roasted them in his open fire in a few weeks. The peas he picked yesterday will taste sweet as they filled his belly that night. The hearty broth and the simple bread he baked was all he would need that day. The fire would still be crackling in the grate as it died down in the early hours, and he would sleep well tonight and rise early to begin another day.

When you have finished with your daydreaming, you need to get to your feet and move off up the slight incline away from the hamlet and towards Carr Road. Cross over the main road and you will approach another fine lodge of the Thornhill Estate.

The Lodge, Carr Lodge, was the second of the four lodges built just after 1850. The road from Carr Lodge was called Eleanor Drive, after Thomas Thornhill's second daughter, Eleanor Frances. You are to take the road to the right, Clara Drive, in order to walk along part of the famed Calverley cutting.

This wide avenue is lined by massive detached houses all private and secluded behind gated entrances. Walk along here for a short distance before passing by the rear of Ferncliffe, now used as a Cheshire home. In only a few hundred yards you reach a small bridge spanning the cutting. Below in a deep ravine you can see the steep sides of Calverley Cutting. A short footpath to the side allows you to leave Clara Drive and descend downwards into the cutting.

Calverley Cutting was created in 1856 by the Thornhill family to replace the old packhorse track through Calverley to Apperley Bridge. It was a passage blasted through the deep rocks and some local people at the time complained that it was too hard for "sickly folk" to navigate. Upon landing in the cutting from above you may be glad it runs downhill from there.

As you stand in the centre of the cutting feel the raw spookiness of the place. It may be only mid-afternoon and the sun may be high and bright in the sky but the cutting does emit a feeling of pure malevolence. Down there on the floor, it seems like midnight but up above the sun still shines. It really is a weird place.

On each side the high craggy rocks tower above blotting out the sun everywhere but the sky above. Thick dense trees grow from the rocks and ivy rolls down the rocks to form a carpet around you. The walls of stone seemed to close in on you and the sense of oppression is almost too much to comprehend. You have no time to imagine men and horses toiling up and down the cutting pulling the stone on the wooden bogies to the canal below. You have to walk downwards through the long chamber of darkness to escape and see the sun once again.

Hoping that nothing or no one jumps down on you from the heights above you squint at the tiny sliver of light that you can see at the bottom of this unholy place. Steel yourself, breath deeply and started to march like Colonel Nicholson in The Bridge on the River Kwai and hope for the best.

Ten minutes later, you will be sat on a rock in the sunshine thanking whatever God it was that gave me safe passage through the cutting that day.

Now you need to cross Harrogate Road and walk towards The George and Dragon public house. Standing proudly opposite the stone bridge over the River Aire, this former Coaching Inn dating from 1587 is currently a Grade I listed building. Engraved on a lintel over a fireplace in an upstairs bedroom are the words "Not for the purpose of making a show but of necessity Samuel Hemmingway and Mary his wife enlarged this house AD 1704. These things are cherishing; victuals, drink, warmth, shelter, which of thou possess, remember to gratefully give thanks to God".

After navigating Calverley cutting you may need to do just that. A pint of Wobbly Bob in the beer garden and the warm sun on your head could appear to be a very good idea as you wait for the 747 Yorkshire Tiger bus to take you back along Harrogate Road towards Bradford Interchange to complete your journey.

City Centre to Tong Village via Raikes Lane

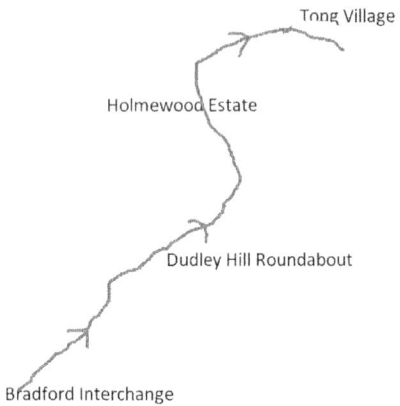

This walk is a mixture of urban sprawl and pastoral countryside. It begins in Bradford Interchange after you have travelled in from wherever it is you live and ends far out in the surrounding countryside after a distance of 5.6 miles.

Leaving the Interchange behind you head for nearby Wakefield Road to start your journey. Wakefield Road is one of the main arteries running out of the city centre and it will take you to the ancient Roman road of Tong Street. From there you can escape the inner city industrial grime and once again immerse yourself in open countryside.

Almost immediately you arrive at the location of the long-gone Adolphus Street Railway Station. Part of the station wall is visible at the junction with Dryden Street on your left. This station stopped serving passengers before even your Grandfather was born never mind your Dad.

In the heady mid-Victorian days of railway fever, Bradford had no less than three terminus stations operated by three different companies; Kirkgate station (later Market Street, then Forster Square), operated by the Leeds & Bradford Railway (LBR), Exchange station, operated by the Lancashire & Yorkshire Railway (LYR) and Adolphus Street station, operated by the Leeds, Bradford & Halifax Junction Railway (LBHJR).

The terminus at Adolphus Street was well laid out and spacious but was inconveniently placed. It was further out of the city centre than the other termini, and passengers had to endure a steep uphill climb to reach the station.

The station was provided with a substantial train shed over six lines. There were four platform faces made up of two side platforms and a central island. Between each pair of platform lines, there was a central road for running round and a concourse at the west end of the train shed. At the back of here was a substantial range of office and passenger facilities including waiting rooms, a telegraph office, and the booking office. The facility also had a goods yard to the east of the station with numerous sidings, two of which passed through a substantial goods shed. There was also a large coal depot on the north side of the yard with an engine shed, turntable and coaling stage on the south side of the goods yard.

The main station building was demolished in the 1970s to allow for the realignment of Wakefield Road. The access ramp to the goods yard on Dryden Street still exists, together with a substantial part of the sidewall, including a bricked-up entrance. This remaining section of wall still looks as good today as the day it was first laid by the hard-working mid-Victorian stonemasons.

The heavy modern wagons thunder up the road alongside oblivious to this superb piece of history. Only a short distance further along Wakefield Road you pass the Railway Club which as the name implies is a nod to the former station. Walking steadily up the gradient of the road you continue towards Tong Street. The area here was distinctly industrialised and showed a certain level of deterioration. Side streets of tightly packed back to back houses peeled off from the far side. These fine old built to last houses have seen better days now but they still offer accommodation to the great unwashed of today.

Shortly you pass under a box section former railway bridge that spans the road. The line it served is long gone but the fenced off bridge remains although access is impossible due to the razor wire around its edges. Up ahead on the left you will see QSS Aquarium Centre. This is housed in a former Police Station and looks good for another few years yet

From here the tall straight spire of St. Johns Church of Bowling beckons you towards it. The clock on the spire seems to wink at you and invite you to sit on the stone steps. Continue up along Wakefield Road and only a few yards past the church you may notice a few moss-covered old stone steps at the side of the pavement. These steps once belonged to a whole series of shops that once stood here on what now is waste ground. There was even a quite sizeable swimming bath situated here until the whole row was demolished sometime in the 1960s.

Modern industrial units and massive roadside advertising hoardings pass by as you continue up Wakefield Road. These give way to a small row of early 18th century cottages at the junction with Fenby Avenue. Standing proud amongst the industrial wasteland these sandstone buildings are a timely reminder to Bradford's heritage.

As you approach Dudley Hill roundabout you need to negotiate the subway to emerge on the other side. Here you stand opposite a quite marvellous if little-known building which stands on the far side. The former Dudley Hill Picture House may today be a mere carpet warehouse but you don't have to look closely to quite easily appreciate its former stylish purpose.

Designed by Cleckheaton Architects Howarth and Howarth for Walter and Percy Goodall, this red brick fronted gem stands alone in a surrounding sea of urban industrial decay. The Goodall brothers had four other cinemas; The Picture Palace in Heckmondwyke, The Pavilion in Dewsbury and The Picture Palace and The Savoy picture House in Cleckheaton. Howarth & Howarth had previously worked for the Goodall's on their other cinemas and came up with a superior design of red brickwork combined with white faience type decoration of LEFCO 'Marmo' tiles made by the Leeds Fireclay Company.

The interior featured a raked (sloping) floor, tip-up seats with better quality seats at the rear and in the small balcony. Goodall was quite ahead of his time by instructing his architects to include a sloping floor in all his cinemas. The Goodall's also claimed to be the first to use 'bucket' seats in their cinemas for better comfort. The vaulted ceiling with plaster moulded decoration led to a similarly curved proscenium arch approximately thirty feet wide with a stage depth of about ten feet. The interior plasterwork was by John Theabold & Sons of nearby Wakefield Road.

The stalls seating capacity of almost six hundred was arranged in two blocks with centre and side aisles with the front row fourteen feet and six inches from the screen. The straight-fronted circle was unusual in that the projection room was in the middle thus dividing the circle into two parts with five rows of seats each side of projection room - a total of just 88 seats.

The first film to be shown at Dudley Hill was "How's Your Father", a black and white American film on the 9th December 1912. The final film to be shown was "Thunderbirds Are Go" and it closed on Saturday 1st April 1967. The premises were then sold to a new owner for use as a Bingo club, but when that ceased the building was unused for a time prompting one Fred Atkinson, Curator of the Beamish Open-Air Museum, to consider the possibility of dismantling the cinema brick-by-brick and re-erecting at Beamish for further use as a cinema.

Sadly the idea did not develop and it became the present-day carpet shop. Despite these two diverse occupancies, the Picture Palace building remains virtually unaltered and is a time capsule of a 1912 vintage picture house.

Leaving this fantastic building behind you continue along Tong Street, passing by the site of the former Dudley Hill Railway Station on the junction with Knowles Lane. This station served The Leeds, Bradford and Halifax Junction Railway and opened to passengers on 20th December 1856 and to goods traffic on 1st January 1857. The station closed in 1952 but passenger services continued on the line until 4th July 1966. Today the site is occupied by a series of industrial units. This station was but one of many in the Bradford area that no longer exists today.

You are now entering an area that once contained many small coal pits, factories, mills, and foundries. It will have been a veritable vision of hell in Victorian times. Today many of the mills survive as industrial units but the coal pits are long gone and resigned to the history books.

Passing by the only pub left on Tong Street, The Holme Lane, you turn down Holme Lane itself a little further on the left to wander past the edge of Holmewood Council Estate to hopefully reach some airy and welcoming countryside beyond.

Rows of dirty early 19th-century terrace houses mingle with giant mills along the roadside. Sprinkled with the odd cottage it seemed very much a miss-matched area. By this point you may be looking forward to the open fields and country lanes that are thankfully not far away.

The unmistakable style of 20th-century social housing becames evident as you continue down Holme Lane. Skirting the estate you come to a long bank of thick bushes along the roadside to your left. A gap opens in the bushes and through here you can see a great expanse of open land.

This was the site of Tong Colliery's massive Number One pit. This pit and numerous other small pits were served by its own tramway which ran between two engine houses, one quite a distance back on Tong Street and the other on Tong Lane close to the village.

Holme Lane had now taken on a distinct countryside feeling, and at the junction with Raikes Lane, you will notice a tiny babbling beck running under an earth banking at the roadside. Filled with new energy and optimism your pace quickens as you pass the old and historic Raikes Hall farmhouse. This late 17th century two-storey farmhouse of coursed Gritstone is today home to a famed riding stable and carriage hire centre. Stop for a while to watch the horses being trained in the fields alongside the farmhouse if you can.

As you turn away from this exhibition of equine excellence your gaze will fall upon another of this area's magnificent and historic residences. Constructed in 1669 on the site of an older timber-framed house, Ryecroft Hall has a south-facing entrance with five mullioned windows, some retaining their original leaded glazing. Inside it even boasts its own original 17th-century Minstrels gallery similar to the one in The Stansfield Arms pub at Apperley Bridge.

From here you continue walking down Raikes Lane following Kit Wood Beck as it trickles alongside you. The water was stained with the familiar tinge of orange from the ironstone that was disturbed by the activities at the many local coal pits. This phenomenon is widespread amongst the watercourses in the Bradford area.

Raikes Lane has narrowed considerably at this point and is flanked on each side by wide open fields and meadows. Stout fences kept the grazing cattle and sheep in their rightful places as the odd isolated cottage flashes by.

The comforting aroma of muck spreading may fill your nostrils as the farmer contentedly works his magic upon the fields some distance away. The hedgerows are alive with tiny birds fluttering and making nests for their young. Out here in places like this time can stand still if you want it to. It is hard to believe you are but a mere three miles from Bradford city centre.

Here you take the right turning off Raikes Lane and start up the long and steep ancient packhorse trail of New Lane. The lane narrows once again as it climbs the hill towards the farmstead of Calverley Clough and Shackleton Wood. The tiny trail was fringed by tall Hawthorne bushes for perhaps half a mile then broke out into wonderful open countryside once again. The surface is broken and uneven after centuries of use by the merchants that walked this route to ply their trade and make their living long ago.

Calverley Clough was the first building of any kind you will have come across for perhaps two miles. The farmyard is open to the road, the yard awash with the evidence of recent cattle movements perhaps. The comforting smell of beasts and nature is all around you. It invades your senses like an old friend, the calling of cattle in a nearby shed fills your ears. Stirring yourself you walk on towards Shackleton Wood. Along with the nearby Park Wood, this forms the boundary of The Tong Park Estate.

By far the largest open space within this area is Tong Park which covers much of the north side of Tong Lane. It is known that prior to the remodelling of Tong Hall in 1773, there was a formal garden directly in front of the building, bounded by high stone walls, with a similarly enclosed garden to the rear. Tong Park surrounded the Hall and is gardens and probably took the form of a grid of pathways bounded by formal planting and lawns. It is unknown whether the remodelling of Tong Hall also involved large-scale changes to the nature of the surrounding parkland, but it is known that the square front and rear garden walls were demolished, meaning the Park itself became the setting for this unique landmark building.

During the last century, the Park covered an area of 32 acres, but under the ownership of Eric Towler between 1941 and 1943, 20 acres of the Park was given over to pasture, leaving a reduced area of formal parkland in the vicinity of the Hall, which by this time had probably lost much of its rigid grid layout.

Today, Tong Park provides an attractive mixture of well-maintained areas of grassland and woodland which provides Tong Hall with an attractive setting. The boundary wall and railings to the Park at Tong Lane are beneath the canopy of densely packed sycamore trees. The gateway is set behind a neatly tapered grass verge which contrasts with the tightly packed wall of foliage on the other side which makes for an interesting tunnel-like vista of Tong Hall, situated some 200m from the gateway.

Passing through the gateway a regular line of shrubbery below the canopy of the deciduous woodland reinforces the straight line of the drive and encloses it. The entrance lodge and the large rectangular fishpond behind it are the only interruptions to the woodland but are more or less swamped by branches and leaves.

But you see none of that as you continue on along New Lane past the farm of Gil Stubbing and the tiny wood named The Shrog. The road widens a little at this point and the flatness of the terrain is welcome after the long haul up from Raikes Lane. Before long you reach the junction with Tong Lane and turn left to head towards the ancient and historic village of Tong. After only a few hundred yards we came to The Old Vicarage.

Built in 1739 this beautiful Grade II listed building has the usual mullioned windows and inside boasts part panelled walls and window seats. The nearby St. James Church was not deemed large enough by the then Lord of the Manor to have a full-time Vicar so the house was lived in by the Curate.

The site of St. James Church, Tong has been a place of Christian worship for close on a thousand years. The church as it stands was rebuilt in 1727 by a team of stonemasons that included John Nelson. Nelson was later to experience a dramatic conversion through the preaching of John Wesley in London and became a significant Methodist leader and preacher. The re-building was instructed by Sir George Tempest of Tong Hall, who had rebuilt Tong Hall in 1702, and was to later build the Village School (now the 'Schoolroom'). The church replaced an earlier building that had been built in c. 1140 A.D.

The Tempest family continued to live at nearby Tong Hall (rebuilt in 1702) until 1941. They were the Lords of the Manor of Tong, and they owned most of the village and surrounding farms. In 1980, during an extensive restoration of the church building, important archaeological discoveries were made which showed that there had been a Saxon church building on the site before the Norman church of 1140.

The foundations of this early church were uncovered and its rough shape identified. The archaeologists also found fragments of Roman pottery and a flint barbed and tonged arrowhead from Bronze Age times. This latter confirmed the likelihood of there having been some kind of settlement here for close on 3,000 years.

There was little change to the life and fabric of the church during the Victorian era. Bell ringing continued to be popular, and the present stained glass window at the East wall was added. The Church is a Grade 1 listed building and is visited by large numbers of people, especially in the summer period. The interior of the church is largely the same as when it was re-built in 1727, and so includes a Georgian style three-decker pulpit, and box pews.

Across the road from the church you will notice a set of double-sided stone steps pushed up against the surrounding church wall. They formed what would have been a mounting block for the carriages of the day, although this was probably not their original position.

Perhaps they had been there the day Alice Tempest married her young rich lover at St James church in Victorian times.

The dark carriage drawn by four shining fine horses stops in front of the church. With a steady hand, the driver brings them to a steady halt by the block. His accomplice jumps down to open the door for the bride. Decked in her beautiful and fine white wedding dress she waits until he opens the door.

The church entrance is surrounded by the invited well to do guests. A sprinkling of local village well-wishers stand gathered. Her father offers his hand to hers and helps his daughter step down from the carriage. The Groom waits nervously inside the church with his best man. Vicar John McStay stands hands clasped in front of him nodding respectfully as he greets the bride. As the group follows the Vicar inside, the watching Poacher with the Jack Russell touches his flat black cap before melted away into the trees.

From the church you need to walk back along Tong Lane towards Westgate Hill where you can catch the bus back to Bradford interchange to conclude this walk.

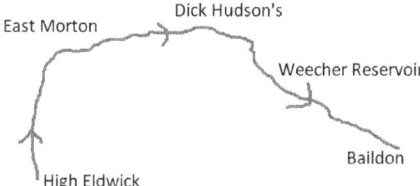

To begin this walk you have to head for Shipley to catch the Eldwick bus that will take you up the slopes of the valley opposite Bingley to the Prince of Wales Park. To reach Shipley you can catch the 612/613/633 buses amongst others from Bradford Interchange. The approximate distance for this walk is 5.2 miles.

From the park you take the next left which is Heights Lane. Heights Lane is long, straight and level which is a good start as you have plenty to see along the way on this walk. Passing by open fields and paddocks with the occasional horse you should make good time. After a short distance, the small number of houses along the roadside fades away to leave an uninterrupted view of fields over both sides.

The disused Height Sandstone quarry flashes by in a moment as you walk the road in silence. Smaller disused quarries like this and tiny old coal pits are dotted all around this area and the wider area of Baildon Moor in general.

You have officially left Eldwick at this point and the drystone walls roll on in splendour as they had done for hundreds of years. Crossing the road and stop to admire the isolated farmhouse and lush mature gardens of Croftlands.

You are now heading towards an area known as The Riggs as you pass the site of the former Bingley Sanitary Tubes and lime works with its associated lime pits to your left. The tall red-brick chimney can be seen from quite a distance and the land around the site is still scared with the evidence of the previous activity.

Further over to the west past this area, you can see Deer Park, a small wooded area where Deer will have roamed since antiquity and most likely still do. Although you are climbing upwards towards The Riggs the gradient was only a gradual increase.

The signpost says one and three-quarter miles back to Bingley but you appear to be in the middle of nowhere such is the seclusion and isolation at this point. On your right you now pass by Drake Hill Cottages, the stone gateposts give Harfleet as its more contemporary name.

The junction with Otley Road is not far away when you pass Prospect House and looking across to your right you can see the banking of the massive Graincliffe Reservoir. Lower down the hillside the smaller Compensation Reservoir is fed from here via Eldwick Beck. This reservoir also controls the flow of water into Loadpit Beck as it flows to its journey's end at the river Aire far below. The modern buildings of the filter beds stand in sharp contrast with rising Baildon Moor far beyond.

You have now reached the junction with Otley Road and here you turn left down the sharp, winding steep hill towards the ancient village of East Morton. This road has been the site of many traffic accidents and even the odd fatality over the years due to its steep nature. The high drystone wall to the right rises up to further enhance the steepness of this road and you should proceed with caution.

The wonderful row of 18th-century sandstone terrace houses of Alma Terrace stand proudly along the right-hand side just as you enter the village. The seventeen or so houses date from the late 18th century and are marked on the maps from 1889 onwards.

As with many streets in England, they were named after the famous battle of Alma in The Crimean War. The Battle of the Alma (20 September 1854) is usually considered the first battle of the Crimean War (1853–1856) and took place just south of the River Alma in the Crimea. An Anglo-French force under Jacques Leroy de Saint Arnaud and Fitzroy Somerset, 1st Lord Raglan defeated General Aleksandr Sergeyevich Menshikov's Russian army, which lost around 6,000 troops.

Beyond these houses are open fields, and beyond that Botany Mill, Providence Mill and Upper Mill. At this point you must walk to the very end of Alma Terrace and take the footpath alongside the last house which will lead you across the field. The path leads you to a small triangular-shaped piece of patchy scrubland where, according to the 1888 Ordnance Survey map, there once stood a "Hydraulic Ram".

A hydraulic ram, or Hydram, is a cyclic water pump powered by hydropower. It takes in water at one "hydraulic head" (pressure) and flow rate, and outputs water at a higher hydraulic head and lower flow rate. The device uses the water hammer effect to develop pressure that allows a portion of the input water that powers the pump to be lifted to a point higher than where the water originally started. The hydraulic ram is sometimes used in remote areas and the fields between the mills of East Morton and the nearby Alma Terrace could perhaps be termed "remote.

Sadly nothing that could fit the description remains today so you return to the footpath once again and walk back to Otley Road to begin the climb out of the village.

At least from here it is a straight and level road as you walk along past the wood of Little Graincliff and Cabin Hill before arriving at the famous public house named Dick Hudson's. Formally known as The Fleece, this pub takes its name from a previous Landlord named Dick Hudson. Situated on the old packhorse trail from Ilkley to Bingley it was a resting place for weary travellers just as it is today.

It was originally a tavern attached to an old farmhouse called The Ploughboy which lost its licence when the new Eldwick road was built. The first Landlord was Thomas Hudson in 1809 and he was succeeded by his Son Dick who held the licence from 1850 to 1878.

Otley Road takes you right past Dick Hudson's and on towards Harvey Smith's farm and horse training centre at Craiglands Farm. Harvey Smith is a well known local Showjumper famous for his "V" sign. He stood out from the ranks of showjumpers because of his broad accent and blunt manner. His career was often controversial; in 1971, he was disciplined (overturned on appeal) after he gave a "V sign" to the judges following a near perfect round which won him the British Show Jumping Derby for the second year in succession.

Opposite the pub Eldwick Crag and its disused quarry rises up like a demon on one side with open fields on the other as you navigate the busy road with great care. Here you pass by a couple of roadside barns and cottages before reaching Eldwick's first Methodist Mission Room and Sunday school. This beautiful tiny building dating from 1815 stands right on the roadside and looks as good today as the day it was built. On the hillside just above this building once stood the wonderfully named residence of Hog Hall. Today only a few stones lay on the hillside as evidence of this fantastically named dwelling.

The moorland falls away to reveal open land and fields on both sides as you approach Smith's Craiglands Farm. The flat land across the road from his farm is ideal galloping and training land for his horses and Lou and you may be fortunate enough to be able to stop and observe a group of them for a while.

Just a short distance past Harvey Smith's place you turn right off the main Otley Road and head down the track alongside Weecher Reservoir. There will be no traffic from here to the end of the walk at the foot of Baildon Moor so you can relax a little and enjoy the passing scenery. The narrow country lane snakes down the side of the vast body of water high above. The high banking and stout wall keep it in place and before long you arrive at Little London Farm.

In centuries past this place was an important meeting place for traders and salt markets were sometimes held on a flat plateau of land below. All through history the availability of salt has been pivotal to civilization. The word "salary" comes from the Latin word for salt because the Roman Legions were sometimes paid in salt, which was quite literally worth its weight in gold.

In Britain, the suffix "-wich" in a place name means it was once a source of salt, as in Sandwich and Norwich.

You are now on Sconce Lane and this will take you to your journey's end. Flanked on one side by tiny disused delphs, the narrow lane winds along through the countryside to take you to Faweather.

In the 13th century, the land for many miles around belonged to the Monks of Rievaulx Abbey. They built the original Grange on this site to serve their medieval estates. The Monks also farmed Sheep on the surrounding hills for their milk, meat, and highly prized fleeces. There is evidence too of iron workings nearby dating from the 13th century.

The lane leads you past Great Wood, Gill Beck, and Faweather Quarry. This quarry was operational from the early 18th century and stone was carted from here to Otley for church building. Like many other small local quarries, it became disused at the end of World War I.

Passing Ash House Farm you now head towards the former hamlet of Sconce itself. This collection of thirteen cottages was built in the mid-18th century for local miners but was reduced to just one in 1934. Many of the small hamlets in this area were demolished by Baildon Council due to sanitation concerns. Today it is owned by Shipley and Baildon Scout Council and used for camping purposes.

Here you may notice a small square of land opposite the site of the cottages at Sconce. Marked "Aviary" on the Ordnance Survey maps it is perhaps the size of half a football pitch and is surrounded all the way round by a drystone wall. A small metal gate gives you access to what appears to be simply a patch of tree-lined grass. The maps do seem to indicate the presence of a small building in the centre with spokes radiating outwards to the outer walls.

This was an artificial hatchery to produce bird eggs for exhibitions. Owned by a Mr Lambert he employed Mr and Mrs Allpress to relocate from Peterborough in 1904 to manage it for him. Later it became a small holiday camp until it burned down in the 1930s.

From this point it is but a short walk before you arrive at the end of Sconce Lane at the point where it meets Hawksworth Road. Turn right here to start the climb up the moor side towards Baildon village where you can catch the 626 bus back into Shipley to conclude this walk.

Today's walk is quite special. You are to visit and walk along one of the Victorians greatest feats of engineering, not just in this area but in any area. The gargantuan edifice that is Thornton Railway Viaduct stands proudly alongside Salts Mill and Listers Mill as marvellous monuments to the Victorians ingenuity and expertise even to this present day.

You start this walk at Keelham crossroads and to reach there you have to take the number 67 Keighley bus from Bradford Interchange. The approximate distance for this walk is 3.2 miles.

The wide-open expansive fields spread out on each side as you leave Keelham crossroads, dotted only with the occasional farm as you stride along the kerbside towards the historic village of Thornton.

Thornton is a village with a rich history of mills, railways and not least the famous Bronte family. The Rev Patrick Brontë became the incumbent of Thornton Chapel in 1815, and Charlotte, Branwell, Emily and Anne Brontë were born at 74, Market Street, Thornton before the family moved to Haworth.

The remains of the church where the father preached, known as the Bell Chapel, can be seen in the restored old graveyard off Thornton Road opposite the current church.

The preserved centre of the village retains the character of a typical Pennine village, with stone-built houses with stone flagged roofs. The surrounding areas consist of more modern housing, still isolated from the rest of the city by green fields. Its elevation, poor soils, isolation from major transport routes, and rainfall of over 34 inches a year limited farm production. Resources such as coal, iron and sandstone, the development of turnpike roads, and the coming of the railways enabled Thornton to share in the prosperity generated by the 19th-century wool worsted trade.

The increasing use of steam-powered mills (at the expense of the former cottage-industry production methods) concentrated production in the valleys of the city centre. Foreign imports, the Second World War, and closure of the railways, all contributed to the decline in manufacturing. Today Thornton is a residential suburb of Bradford but still retains some wonderful cottages dating back to the dawn of the Industrial Revolution.

Walking along the main road towards Thornton you soon pass the farmstead of Lower Bottomley Holes and the imaginably named cottages Top of the Row. At Pearson Place stop for a minute to admire the crumbling roadside shell of a former warehouse. Today it appears sad and forlorn with its boarded-up windows and half its roof missing. The rotting wooden boom above the upper loading bay windows hang out from the building like the Grim Reapers thin boney finger apportioning blame to those who had abandoned the building.

Continuing on from here and almost immediately you can see the upper rampart of a railway bridge across the road. The line passed underneath Thornton Road at this point to carry the line into the southern entrance portal of Well Heads Tunnel. Glancing over the wall on your side of the road you can also see the deep tree-filled cutting which leads to the portal. Here a small path runs through the undergrowth and if you are feeling energetic you could perhaps leap over the wall and drop down to see how far it goes.

The portal entrance is only just visible and you can see it is bricked up with hefty metal gates securing it. A shame as a visit to the inside of a Victorian railway tunnel is always a treat due to the magnificent largely preserved stonework that is usually found within.

Constructed between 1878-1881, the tunnel boasts a vaulted stone roof and stone portals and buttressed sides but contains no airshafts. When built this tunnel was some 662 yards long but the removal of the northern portal has reduced this by forty yards. The inside contains regular refuges in the walls and on one grim stormy evening some years ago a man was found dead huddled up inside refuge number thirteen.

The line was closed to passenger trains in 1955 but remained open for goods traffic until 1961. From the direction and layout of the tunnel and line, you can judge that the former station and viaduct lay on the south side of the main road so you have an inkling of the direction that you should be taking when you enter the village.

The road is long and straight as you approach Simmonites Land Rover dealership. Opposite here stands the massive and impressive Thornton Cemetery with its seventeen Commonwealth War Graves. A track up the side of the graveyard leads past an old abandoned water Filter House then onto the Bottom of the Row farmstead.

The Filter House was built in 1926 by Bradford County Waterworks to serve the villages of Denholme and Thornton before closing in 1975. Most of the tucked away farms in this area have wonderful and evocative sounding names, Top and Bottom of the Row are but two and another named simply Squirrel can be found not far away.

From here the open fields turn into rows of roadside bungalows and houses. Mostly late Victorian houses of a middle-class nature on one side with the odd rundown warehouse on the other. You are now entering the built-up area on the edge of the village. The road to your right falls away to reveal the gully where Pinch Beck runs. Beyond that, the distant hills climbed up towards Queensbury and the windswept hamlet of Mountain. There is your journeys end after you have sampled the delights of a walk along the viaduct and the former railway trackbed.

Turn around at this point and look back along the road that you have walked along. Perhaps a thousand yards away you can just make out the trees around the southern portal for Well Heads tunnel. The fields between the trees climb up towards Close Hill Lane where the northern end of the tunnel broke through the heavy soil.

You have now entered the village of Thornton and this is apparent due to the build-up of the roadside housing. Look across the road and you can see cobbles and stone walls that are the only remaining signs of the Thornton Railway Station. No other parts of this large station remain.

The station had an island platform and was reached from the road by a fifty-foot iron bridge. The site has been occupied by Thornton Primary School (previously Royd Mount Middle School) since 1977. The original goods platform and a large retaining wall are still visible and have been incorporated into the school's grounds design.

The area of the goods yard is now occupied by the school's playing field. A large stone warehouse measuring 130 feet by 50 feet once stood here. It handled coal, wood, livestock and animal feeds. It is down the side of the school via a pathway that you gain access to the viaduct.

Thornton Viaduct opened in 1878 as part of the Great Northern's route from Queensbury to Keighley - arguably, the most engineered section of railway in West Yorkshire. It is Grade II listed, incorporates 20 barrel-vaulted arches - each with a span of 40 feet - and its 300-yard length incorporates a rare S-shaped curve to allow access to Thornton Station.

The old trackbed crosses Pinch Beck at a height of 120 feet. The structure is formed of 17,000 cubic yards of masonry as well as 750,000 bricks. It is supposedly haunted by the ghost of "Fair Becca", who fell from her horse whilst riding along the top of the viaduct. Local folklore says that if you call her name three times she will appear.

Upon finding the path down the side of the school you can start to walk along the former trackbed on the top of the viaduct. From here the vista of Pinch Beck Valley and the golf course below is stunning, the stonework unrivalled in its complexity. Seven hundred and fifty thousand stone bricks held together with mortar and Victorian sweat.

You walk the tarmac former rail bed as the viaduct curves along the contours of the valley. From here you can clearly see Lister's Mill and its fine chimney far away amongst the bustle of Bradford city centre. The bright green dome of its neighbouring Mosque shines in the early afternoon sunlight. Away to your right are the hills leading upwards to Queensbury and it is there that you are now walking towards.

It may be only two miles away but it appears a lot further as the viaduct ends and the track towards the massive High Birks Embankment begins.

Before reaching the embankment you arrive at Upper Headley Hall. This fine unaltered hall was built by the Midgley family in the reign of Elizabeth I in 1589. Constructed of coursed Gritstone and stone slate roofs this building has a gabled west wing of moulded Saddle stone. The front entrance has a particularly good square of chamfered mullioned transom windows which most unusually retain their original leaded glazing and wrought iron casements. The interior retains tarred oak doors and panelled partitioning.

Almost immediately you are along the top of High Birks Embankment. This 104 feet long, 900 feet long structure was constructed from 250,000 yards of tipping material dug out from the nearby tunnels. Constructed to span the Birks valley below subsidence was a huge problem for the Victorian engineers when it was built.

Crossing over Cockin(g) Lane, the trail is flat and the surrounding countryside just purrs by. Crows and Magpies shake the nearby treetops when you rouse them from their slumbers.

You are now approaching the famous "Queensbury Railway Triangle". You have been walking along the former track that took the line over Thornton viaduct and on to Keighley. The Queensbury Lines was the name given to a number of railway lines in West Yorkshire, England that linked Bradford, Halifax, and Keighley via Queensbury. All the lines were either solely owned by the Great Northern Railway (GNR) or jointly between the GNR and the Lancashire and Yorkshire Railway (L&YR).

The lines opened piecemeal from 1879 and it was not until 1882 that a full service was available. Passenger services continued until 1955, most goods services continued until the 1960s and the final part of the line to close lasted until 1972.

The lines were marked with a number of major civil engineering works including several viaducts and tunnels. A feature of the line was the unusual station at Queensbury which until the latter part of the 20th century was one of only two stations in the United Kingdom that consisted of a triangular junction with platforms on all three lines forming the junction.

It boasted a triangular layout with inner and outer platforms on all three sides, as well as a signal box at each corner. The first train pulled in during the spring of 1879. The line north snaked its way to Keighley, embracing viaducts, tunnels and lofty views over the industrial sprawl - earning it the affectionate title of 'The Alpine Route'. To the south-west, via the glorious gloom of Queensbury tunnel, lay Halifax whilst Bradford nestled to the east, also linked by a hole through the hill.

Much to the annoyance of locals, Queensbury itself was perched high above its station, connected by a steep, meandering lane which the Great Northern Railway grudgingly lit after some protest. Today, the triangle has lost its shape and the platforms have been engulfed by twenty feet of landfill. A lonely rusting footbridge rests below the station house, next to the spot where the signal box once stood.

Today the tunnel underneath Queensbury is blocked by metal gates. This tunnel was opened in July 1878 when the link to Halifax was completed. The tunnel was 2501 yards long and almost a quarter of a mile under the village of Queensbury. It was the longest tunnel on the Great Northern rail system and took nearly four years to complete. Queensbury itself stands on top of the hill the tunnel cuts through, part of it about 1,000 feet above sea level.

Apart from its unusual platform arrangement Queensbury station had a sheer drop of over 50 feet behind one platform. When seen from this side it had rather a Swiss appearance, fostered perhaps by the massive timber supports on the steep hillside. As a change from tunnels, the Keighley line beyond Queensbury provided passengers with some wonderful open views from Thornton Viaduct. By 1970, only the degraded remains of the platforms and station subway under the Halifax to Keighley platforms could be seen.

Apart from the rusting metal footbridge the only visible remains today is the former Station house nearby. Even the subway was demolished in 2004 and the valuable Yorkshire stone spirited away for use in other building projects.

Look for a broken gravestone in the centre of the triangle. It belonged to John Dalby who worked for The Midland Railway for forty years. The 1881 census tells us that John Dalby was married, age 64, a Railway Canvasser that lived at number 66, Four Lane Ends in Bradford. He was buried at St John the Baptist in Clayton. But exactly why his headstone rested here amongst the tall grass at the former site of the Queensbury railway triangle is a mystery.

Leaving the former railway triangle, you make your way up Station Road and then take a footpath which would bring you out onto the main Bradford Road at Scarlet Heights. During the hike uphill, you can appreciate just how the locals felt when the station was built down in the valley. Lugging bags and trunks up the gradient will have tested even the most athletic and agile late Victorians.

No doubt the station forecourt was filled with horse-drawn cabs every night as the trains pulled into this strange and unusual station. The final stretch of the day up to Scarlet Heights will test you but the view from the top as you look back down into the triangle and across the valley to Thornton is well worth it.

You can rest your aching limbs on the 576 bus from Scarlet heights down into Bradford or Halifax to complete this walk.

This walk begins at the junction of Kings Road and Queens Road in Manningham. It is an inner-city ramble amongst the somewhat decaying examples of Victorian and Edwardian architecture, the pastoral pleasures that are described elsewhere in this book are far away.

To reach the starting point you can catch the 612/613/614/633/747 buses from Bradford Interchange. The approximate distance for this walk is 4. 1 miles.

The first stop is the site of the former Manningham Railway Station on Queens Road. Today this place is a stone reclamation yard and the only remains that can be seen is the station perimeter wall running along North Avenue. The station opened on February 17th, 1868 and was the first stop on the Leeds and Bradford branch line of the Midland Railway as it left Forster Square Station. Although today this station is known as Forster Square, in the days of Manningham Station it was known as The Midland Station after the company who ran the line.

The opening of the station brought the middle classes to live in the area during the textile boom in the late 1800s when English and German textile merchants moved in. It was quite a huge site in the days when Bradford was known as "Worstedopolis" and it was the centre of the world's Woollen manufacturing industry.

From 1872, there was an extensive network of sidings and sheds to the north of Manningham Station and it was a hive of much activity. The Station Masters house stood across Queens Road where the Enterprise car rental company now have an office. The station closed due to the Beeching axe on the 20th March 1965 and although there have been recent plans to resurrect a station on the site nothing has so far come of it.

From here you continu up Queens Road towards Manningham and almost immediately you will notice a decline in the general appearance of the area. The once proud and immaculate terraced houses lining the road are somewhat scruffy and degraded, the pavement is littered with general detritus. It seems there are empty Cannabis bags every five paces and coke cans every ten.

You hike up the steep gradient and cross over Manningham Lane to continue on towards Carlisle Road. Just for a fleeting moment the scruffiness of the area is lifted when the quite magnificent Apsley Crescent came into view on your left. Built for wealthy middle-class Bradfordians the twenty-four houses on this curved terrace were designed in fashionable classical and Italianate styles by Architects Andrews and Delaunay and constructed in 1855. Your spirits may be lifted when you see one of the few curved terraces left in Yorkshire. Apsley Crescent would not look out of place in the great city of Bath.

Turning off along Church Street, you will experience more poor quality housing and even more poor quality roadsides as you continue on through Manningham.

Even from here you can see the marvellous giant stone chimney of Listers Mill. You are now on the edge of what was once Bradford's famed red light area and one of the haunts of The Yorkshire Ripper Peter Sutcliffe. Opposite Skinner Lane, perhaps stop to admire the former Bradford Children's Hospital. This imposing 1889 Grade II listed stone building with its two storeys "turreted" annex is presently a Mosque for the Muslim Community.

You now turn up Skinner lane then onto Rosebery Road where one of the area's oldest buildings stands. It is also probably the most unloved and destitute buildings of any in Manningham. The Old Manor House was thought to have been built in the early 16th century as a hall and cross-winged timber framed house. This places it in a group thought to represent the type of dwelling adopted by the wealthiest of the Yeomanry. The house has been unoccupied for a number of decades and has fallen into a sad state of repairs.

From this point you now join Oak Lane and turn uphill to walk towards the grand and imposing masterful Victorian building that is Listers Mill. Otherwise known as Manningham Mills it once was the largest Silk factory in the world.

Built by Samuel Cunliffe Lister to replace the original Manningham Mills that were destroyed by fire in 1871, the mill is a Grade II listed building built in the Italianate style of Victorian architecture.

At its height, Lister's employed 11,000 men, women and children and manufactured high-quality textiles such as velvet and silk. It supplied 1,000 yards of velvet for King George V's coronation and in 1976, new velvet curtains for the President Ford's White House. The 1890-91 strike at the mill was important in the establishment of the Independent Labour Party which later helped found the modern-day Labour Party.

On completion in 1873, Lister's Mill was the largest textile mill in North England. Floor space in the mill amounts to 27 acres, and its imposing shape remains a dominant feature of the Bradford skyline. The chimney of the mill is 255 feet high, and can be seen from most areas of Bradford.

The powering of the machinery switched over to electricity in 1934. Before that, huge steam boilers drove the mill. Every week the boilers consumed 1,000 tons of coal which were brought in on company rail wagons from the company collieries near Pontefract. Water was also vital in the process and the company had its own supply network including a large covered reservoir on-site.

During World War II Lister's produced 1,330 miles of real parachute silk, 284 miles of flame-proof wool, 50 miles of khaki battledress and 4,430 miles of parachute cord. Lister's business decreased considerably during the 1980s. Stiff foreign competition and changing textile trends such as increased use of artificial fibres were the reasons.

In 1992, the mills were closed. Being a prominent structure the mills attracted a great deal of attention and several regeneration proposals came and went. The sheer size of the buildings being a major difficulty. In 2000, property developers Urban Splash bought the mills. They planned to renovate the existing larger buildings and build new ones. Apartments, workplaces, shops and public spaces were planned to be part of Listers.

Silk Warehouse, which was completed in 2006, created 131 new homes and the lower ground floor is home to Mind the Gap, a disabled performing arts charity. Velvet Mill is the second phase of the regeneration of Lister Mills. Designed by David Morley Architects, the largest listed building in Bradford has been lovingly restored into new homes and ground floor commercial spaces.

Bursting with original features, Velvet Mill combines the best of the old with the best of the new, and the new dramatic curved rooftop apartments are a fine example of how combining old and new architecture can transform an already magnificent building into a modern-day classic.

If you need an injection of class and culture, the next example is only just around the corner. A short stroll past the red-bricked building of a former Telephone exchange along Heaton Road brings you to a pair of stone gateposts. Beyond these, up a narrow lane are the historic "Tradesmen's Homes".

Termed as Almshouses these buildings were constructed for the benefit of retired local tradesmen and their families who had fallen on hard times. Founded by public subscription in 1867 these houses are arranged around a rectangular green. Local luminaries such as Sir Titus Salt, Sir Isaac Holden, and Samuel Cunliffe Lister were amongst the subscribers to this noblest of projects.

The high Victorian Gothic style buildings were designed by Milnes and France and were constructed of Sandstone brick with Ashlar dressings and steeply pitched Welsh slate roofs. In the centre of the north range is a Chapel and assembly room with stained glass windows and a projecting canted front. Today the homes and their grounds within this beautiful square are immaculate in the extreme and it is a joy to walk around and admire yet another example of the city of Bradford's Victorian benefactor's finest moments.

But sadly as you leave this hidden and almost unknown oasis you have to endure yet more litter-strewn streets lined with closed down takeaway shops and motor factors as you walk further along Heaton Road. All the rows of once fine Victorian terrace houses at this point were built to house the workers at nearby Lister's Mill. They were built to last and that they indeed have but the shabby appearance of most of them is disheartening, to say the least. From one extreme to another you cannot think of any other area that matches Manningham.

At the end of Heaton Road and the junction of Bavaria Place and Church Street stands another forlorn and crumbling sad old building. The ornate Gothic structure of the Old Police Station was built in 1877 and designed once again by famed local architects Milnes and France. The two storeys and attic was constructed in Ashlar Sandstone with Mullioned windows. The most striking feature is the rounded corner tower topped by a steep corniced French roof of fine green slate. Next to this building stood until recently a huge underground reservoir. Contained within an area surrounded by stout stone walls this reservoir has now been dismantled and the site cleared for redevelopment.

On the far side of the reservoir there was once a public toilet situated in the stone wall. Some years ago a local pub barman was bludgeoned to death in there after his shift. Despite a huge Police door to door search, his assailant was never caught, and it became just another of Bradford's unsolved murder mysteries.

From here you continue on and walk on to reach Toller Lane which would take you towards the city centre and the White Abbey area. You pass what was once The Upper Globe public house. The building was, of course, destroyed in the recent riots. Today the building houses a thriving builders merchants business but sadly it is one drinking hole less in the area.

From this point you are now on Whetley Hill moving through a whole avenue of Sari shops, takeaways and carpet shops. Before you turn off Whetley Hill to take City Road you will be right on top of what is most certainly a patch of grass that most people are unaware of.

This large triangular-shaped section of playing field was once home to the original Infirmary of Bradford. Completed in 1844 and extended in 1864 this hospital was in use until it was replaced by today's modern Bradford royal Infirmary on Duckworth Lane in 1936. I

It replaced a Dispensary which was established in 1825 and then moved to Darley Street in 1827. Today there is no trace of the Infirmary apart from some strange stone arches in the stone wall that runs along the far side on Lumb Lane.

Taking City Road for only a few hundred yards, you cross Sunbridge road to join Preston Street. This was an area that is home to the famous back street pub The Fighting Cock. With its Romany style frontage, The Fighting Cock is one of Bradford's hidden gems. Much in the mould of a traditional public house it has been the CAMRA pub of the year on many occasions and rightly so. The ever-changing selection of well-brewed and well-kept hand-pulled beers are a delight to sample.

You are now in Listerhills, once home to many railways and great mills. Many decades ago it was a thriving yet grimy environment and many a great fortune was made here on the sweaty backs of the inner city living working-class people. Images of flat caps, rolled fags in mouth corners and shiny rain-sodden cobbles filled your mind as you walk along past one of the area's finest mills of all.

Designed by another of the districts famous Architect partnerships Lock wood and Mawson, Legrams Mill was a steam-powered Worsted mill. This mill was constructed in 1873 and was originally designed as an integrated mill complete with combing shed, weaving shed, and warehouse. The slump in the fortunes of the traditional Bradford products of Cotton and Worsteds caused the mill to adapt to become a spinning mill and the weaving shed was never built. Today the former mill has been adapted once again to become a series of smart apartments and flats.

Tramping on past row upon row of former mill workers back to back houses you reach the junction with Horton Grange road and turn along here to make your way ever closer to the highlight of this walk.

Here, the road is lined with middle-class Victorian terraced properties with more back to backs spreading out behind. Take a short cut through the back streets here to find yourself on Horton Park Avenue just at the point where the railways used to run.

Today this spot is occupied by the car park for the Mumtaz restaurant nearby. From this point you continue along the road towards Horton Park. This public park was opened on the 25th of May 1878 on land purchased by Bradford Council in 1873. From 1980 to 1932 Horton Park Avenue was served by a tramway which ran alongside the park

The main entrance is set back from the road and is flanked by stone gateposts which support two pairs of late 19th-century ornate iron gates. A few yards to the right stands a two-storey stone lodge which is used as offices by Bradford Council. Just a few yards further back along the road from the lodge is the site of the park's former glasshouses and a fine conservatory. These were removed many years ago but an ornate drinking fountain which once stood in the wall nearby survives, albeit without its fittings and inscription plate.

Almost directly across the road from here is the site of the former Horton Park railway station. This was a station on the Queensbury-Bradford section of the Queensbury Lines which ran between Bradford, Keighley and Halifax via Queensbury. The station was built to serve the nearby football ground. It opened for passengers in 1880 closed for regular passenger trains in 1952 but remained open to special trains on match days until 1955.

The station had a large goods yard which kept it open like the City Road Goods Branch until 1972 when it shut and the tracks lifted. The station remained in place along with its concrete sign until only a few years ago when the station was demolished to make way for the new Al-Jamia Suffa-Tul-Islam Grand Mosque. Today very little apart from part of the stone station wall survives of the railway station.

Perhaps you should sit on the wall outside the Mosque to rest for a few minutes. Then, when refreshed, you should jump down from the wall to join the massed crowd of mainly men as they make their way towards the turnstiles at the Powell Avenue end of the ground.

It is a cold Tuesday afternoon in April 1941 and Avenue are playing a Wartime Cup game against the then mighty Preston North End. The local hero, the "Clown Prince of Soccer" Len Shackleton is playing tonight and you are going to cheer him on with typical teenage gusto from the terraces.

Today you are free to mingle with the large crowd queuing outside the turnstiles to pay your threepenny admission fee tonight. Oh to be able to afford the half a crown to sit in Leitch's fine double-decker stand and watch in comfort. But then you might miss the camaraderie and closeness of your fellow working-class Bradfordians on the packed terraces as Shack twists and turns to beat four Preston defenders to score the winning goal in the last minute. All those flat caps in the air will be a fine sight indeed.

Today The Dolls House and Archibald Leitch's fine old gabled stand has long since disappeared, half of the pitch is now occupied by a fitness centre, and the terrace has sprouted a small forest of trees. The perimeter wall with its occasional bricked up entrances still remains, though, but this is high and topped with barbed wire making any attempt at scaling it a useless exercise.

From the old Park Avenue ground it is a short and uncomplicated walk back into Bradford to catch a bus from the Interchange on towards where ever it is you live.

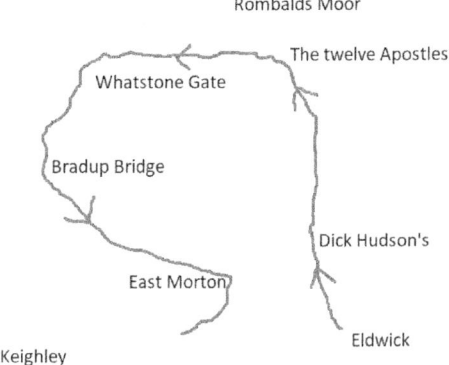

Rombalds Moor

The twelve Apostles

Whatstone Gate

Bradup Bridge

Dick Hudson's

East Morton

Eldwick

Keighley

To begin this walk you must catch bus 619 from Bradford Interchange. The end of the line is Eldwick Beck Bottom and it is here that you leave the bus. The approximate distance for this walk is 4.2 miles

The end of the line is still a short walk through the countryside before you once again reach Dick Hudson's pub on Otley Road. From here you have to walk for a short while on the well-trodden Dalesway Link towards the summit of Bingley Moor.

Crossing the road at the side of the pub you stand at the entrance gate and fill your lungs with air to help propel you up the daunting pathway before you. The path is clearly defined due to the stout drystone walls on either side so it was simply a case of tramping upwards towards the horizon.

After a while the surface of the path changes from random broken half-sunken rocks to flat stones making it easier on your ankles. The bleak open moorland opens up and you must avoid the swampy bog that lines each side of the pathway. Focussed your attention on the tiny milepost on the horizon.

The moorland seems to stretch forever around you as you reach Spy Hill. At one thousand feet above sea level, you have done most of the climbing. Reward your sweaty efforts with a short rest atop a large rock. Although still muddy at least from here the terrain is flat and even. You can now start to enjoy the bleak and windswept Hog Hill Flat.

Images of grizzled old men leading packhorses loaded high with cloth perhaps fill your mind as you pass the milestone that points the way to Ilkley. The track has changed to hard-packed sand at this point and you should start to make good time towards the summit of the moor. Passing through Peat Edge you climb another two hundred and fifty feet as the trail snakes on and on through the banks of heather.

To seasoned moor walkers it may not be the outer edge of nowhere but this area is rather remote and windswept. Eventually after what seems an age you arrive at The Twelve Apostles stone circle on the very top of the moor.

The Twelve Apostles is probably the most visited prehistoric site in West Yorkshire. Dating back to The Bronze Age (2000BC) it is also the most damaged and unfortunately the stones have been moved about quite a bit in the last century. Even so they still attract quite a lot of speculation from different faiths, cults, and religions.

The dozen uprighted stones are just over a metre in height and appear evenly spaced with no obvious entrance to the ring. Descriptions from the 19th century suggest there may have been as many as twenty stones at one time. An earlier earth bank that surrounded the stones is also mentioned. There have been theories that suggest the stones were used to observe the movement of the Moon and other celestial bodies-indeed it was once known as a "Druidical Dial Circle". It is also said that from within the stone circle the rising summer solstice sun appears exactly above the White Horse at Kilburn.

The stones were erected close to the crossing of the two most important trackways crossing these moors, marking an event of some importance. These trackways face the four cardinal points, or airts, and one of them is believed by archaeologists to have been a major prehistoric trade route that crossed the mid-Pennines.

Around 1800 BC – the academics guess – the ring of stones took form. The all-but-forgotten Black Beck Well, two hundred yards south of the Twelve Apostles, was an important water-hole for the prehistoric traders and travellers and may well have had some function relative to this megalithic ring. Certainly, the well was being used by traders late into the 19th century.

One thing is certain, that the circle in front of you today bears little resemblance to the place when it was first constructed around four thousand years ago. The scattered woodland which covered most of these now-barren moorland heights have long since gone and the stones have been moved and overthrown so many times that it would be very difficult indeed to gain an accurate picture of what the circle originally looked like.

Leaving the circle you walk on for a few metres then take a track that runs off to the left. You follow this track across Rombalds Moor towards Whetstone Gate. On the horizon to the west, you can see another tall stone cairn, which is unmissable in this treeless landscape.

A straight line through this cairn will strike The Swastika Stone and is said to mark the point of the major Lunar standstill, the maximum moonrise on the northwestern horizon, an event that only occurs once every nineteen years. Next to this is a Trig point which marks the highest point on the moor. The large stone slabs you are now moving along were laid perhaps only a century ago to prevent soil erosion by the many boots that tramp across this part of the moor.

Continuing along this path you soon pass by an imposing group of boulders known as the Thimble Stones. These appear to have also been a stone circle at one time. Here lie two huge chunks of millstone Grit with a recumbent boulder forming a natural altar. It is quite likely these stones had some relevance to the Prehistoric inhabitants of the moor.

Once past this point the path takes you towards and then along a massive centuries-old dry stone wall on the western boundary of the moor. Apart from the Trig point and the milestone markers, this wall is the first sign of any sort of modern human activity you will have seen since leaving Dick Hudson's. Half a mile further on is Whetstone Gate which marks the former main Keighley to Ilkley road. The name originally denoted the presence of a stone in the area used for the sharpening of knives.

You have now reached Whetstone Gate andyoury attention turns to the small village of East Morton way below. Walking quickly past the small building with its attached Police radio relaying mast you join the narrow tarmac road alongside. This will lead you down to East Morton.

Whetstone Gate is an area north of Riddlesden where a narrow lane leads down towards the beautifully isolated cottage of Bradup and then East Morton beyond. The lower slopes of the moor provide pasture for sheep farming and this gives way to an expanse of heather moorland which forms the southwestern part of Rombalds Moor. This area is rich in bird life with breeding pairs of Meadow Pipit, Skylarks, Lapwings, and Curlews. Birds of prey are also often seen here circling the sky waiting to pounce on their prey.

The road drops quite sharply as you pass the disused and abandoned Whetstone Quarry. Just past this point, at the side of the road, notice a stone drinking trough being filled at a high rate by a natural spring. It carries the inscription "T11 XS 1858". The water is crystal clear and burbles away in the silence of the moor as it fills the trough.

In times of antiquity, any decent source of water was held in high regard and this spot will most certainly have been one of the most revered on the whole moor.

You will see the isolated cottage of Bradup just a short distance down the road. As you approach it notice the series of small enclosures in the field opposite. These were sheep pens where the local sheep which grazed on the moor all their lives would be brought to be sheared of their woollen coats. The thin narrow chambers which constrained them whilst they were being relieved of their fleeces had something of a "Heath Robinson" look about them and it all appeared to be a small scale operation. Artisan craftsmen at their best.

You may find this little area to be beguiling in the extreme. The deserted cottage, Bradup Beck, and its ancient bridge may make you want to stay sat there on the wall for a whole week. Try to imagine what it would be like to live right here in the winter. How isolated, secluded and alone you would be. There would be no Sky TV or Broadband, no mobile connection for your phone. But the fire would glow from the peat blocks you had cut from the nearby moor in the summer and that would be recompense enough.

From Bradup Beck you continue down the road past the rolling heather tinged fields until you reach the farmstead of Upwood. The Roman road from Manchester to Ilkley passed close by here and the most preserved section was broken up by William Busfeild (Busfield) in 1848 and used to construct nearby drystone walls.

After only a few yards you turn left onto Upwood Lane which runs alongside the farm. This is no more than a footpath in reality and will lead you through open fields before eventually reaching the north side of East Morton. Open moorland has now changed to pastoral countryside and for the first time you can smell the familiar aroma of the countryside. Cattle and sheep fill the nearby fields as you make your way along the high walled flanked track. Over to the south is the tiny cosy hamlet of West Morton.

The path turns to skirt along the grounds of Manor Heath. The secluded gardens of this fine house lay behind a massive stone wall that was only interrupted by a small wooden door. A secret door to a secret garden where fairy's and pixies held court amongst the water lilies of the pond perhaps?

Back in the real world, the pathway takes you to Green End Road and disused Upper Mill. This Cotton spinning mill was constructed in 1798 but was destroyed by fire in 1899. This whole area was dotted with cotton, Worsted, and paper mills at one time, a veritable hive of industrial activity all powered by Morton Beck.

Old Side Mill at Alma Hill was built in 1792 and believed to be the first Cotton mill in the area. Sunnydale Mill which manufactured banknotes and stationary was thought to have the biggest waterwheel in Britain at one time. Built in 1833 this mill closed in 1878 and was finally demolished in 1935. The largest mill was the Worsted manufacturing Botany Mill which closed in 1938. Manufactured goods would have been transported to the south of the valley where a warehouse and wharf on the Leeds-Liverpool Canal was conveniently situated.

To house the worker's, rows of 19th-century cottages were constructed near the mill sites. These included Providence Row near Botany Mill and Upper Mill Row adjacent to Upper Mill, and the now demolished cottages near Sunnydale Mill. Alma terrace on Otley Road, built in the 19th century was also owned by Botany Mill.

Despite industrialisation and growth, a number of farmhouses and cottages dating to the 17th and 18th centuries survive to the present day. Some of these are Grade II listed and include Laurel Bank which contains a date stone dated 1669. Situated on the main road, Green End Road similarly contains two surviving farmhouses and cottages of this date, and one farmhouse with a date stone dated 1664.

Today Sunnydale is a place of solitude, however, this cannot be said of the last two hundred years or so. At the end of the 1700s the industrial revolution arrived in East Morton with something of a vengeance with mills and factories springing up all along Morton Beck. This was to take advantage of the ready supply of water from the beck to drive the waterwheels and later the steam engines used to power the mills. Although the worker's cottages can still be seen and indeed are still lived in, the same cannot be said of the mills as these have long since disappeared. Strangely enough, the remains of the engine house at Sunnydale Mill can still be seen hiding amongst the undergrowth.

As you wander around the tiny streets of former mill workers cottages in this area, it will not be difficult to conjure up images of hardy men with whiskers and flat caps coming home after a hard days graft at the local mill. Trudging along the street in their clogs as their children ran along to greet them, it will have been a hard life but one that may have had a meaning that has been lost forever today.

The small Methodist Chapel on Green End Road will have been packed every Sunday with the men and their wives dressed in their finest clothes. The starched white collarless shirts worn by the men only on this day, the bright floral dresses shimmering in the summer sun as the women leave after the sermon.

They were simple people who possessed only simple things.

It is downhill all the way as you walk through the village heading for Morton Lane. This long road winds down the valley side and will take you to Keighley Road where you can once again catch the bus back to Shipley.

Passing by a myriad of old cottages and a handful of grand Victorian houses you cross Morton Swing Bridge near the aqueduct that carries Morton Beck over the canal.

As you sit on the grass beside the bus stop, perhaps mull over what you have seen and experienced on this walk. You have witnessed the ingenuity of industrial man and felt the spirituality of his Prehistoric forefathers all on the same day. You have been on a journey across the ages and through the past in the space of a few hours.

That would make a good song that would lad, aye lad it would.

The Stag's Head Publishing Company (Queensbury) February 2020

The Author can be contacted at montyw111@hotmail.co.uk or
www.facebook.com/markalexanderjacksonhistory/
The Author is also a joint admin of The Facebook group Queensbury
(West Yorkshire) History

Search Amazon for other titles by Mark Alexander Jackson:

The Green Historical Walking Guide to West Yorkshire   2020
A Raggald and a Russell (Walk Through Queensbury's History)   2017

Printed in Great Britain
by Amazon